MW01487176

You Can Throw Harder

An Engineer's Approach
To Developing More Velocity

By

Ken Shuey

© 2001, 2002 by Ken Shuey. All rights reserved.

No part of this book may be reproduced, stored in a retrieval system, or
transmitted by any means, electronic, mechanical, photocopying, recording,
or otherwise, without written permission from the author.

ISBN: 1-4033-0999-X (Hardcover)
ISBN: 1-4033-0998-1 (Paperback)
ISBN: 1-4033-0997-3 (e-book)

This book is printed on acid free paper.

1stBooks - rev. 06/19/02

CONTENTS

ACKNOWLEDGMENTS

I would like to thank the people who were most instrumental in the writing of this book, starting with my immediate family. My wife Bern has offered continued support and encouragement and has been extremely helpful in editing and reviewing the text. She has been consistently patient regarding my requests to review the large number of iterations that have been brought to her for comment.

My younger son Matt has reviewed the book and has provided significant input on hitting techniques that are used for comparison to throwing fundamentals. I want to thank Matt for making himself available as the primary photography subject for demonstrations of the rotator cuff and back exercises in Chapter 12. The majority of these exercises are second nature to Matt after his collegiate baseball experience.

I owe the largest debt of gratitude to my older son Paul who is the primary subject of analysis in the book. Paul has offered many concepts and instruction techniques that are in the book and has continually offered enthusiastic support of the project.

In addition, Paul made contact with Mr. Kenneth Carr, a professional photographer from Cleveland. Paul arranged his spring training schedule to match with Mr. Carr's schedule so that the sequences of pictures in the book could be shot in Winter Haven, Florida. I certainly want to acknowledge my appreciation to Mr. Carr for his efforts and quality work.

Paul also introduced me to Mr. Dell Bethel, an accomplished athlete and author. Mr. Bethel, with Paul's encouragement, was nice enough to review the book and offer insight and guidance that meant a lot in this first book project.

Paul presented the book project to Omar Vizquel and encouraged him to be involved. Mr. Vizquel provided the artistic front cover sketch for the book. Obviously, Mr. Vizquel's talents go beyond the magic that he creates on the baseball diamond and I want to offer my sincere thanks for being involved in the project.

Needless to say, this book would not have been possible without Paul's ability to throw a baseball coupled with his willingness, dedication and energy for this project.

Lastly, I would like to thank Paul and his wife Julie for allowing me to take pictures of my granddaughter, Morgan.

I want to thank John Hart, the previous General Manager of the Cleveland Indians and Mark Shapiro, the present General Manager for approving of the use of Paul's pictures in the Indians uniform.

I also want to thank the two young men, Matt and Chris Ball, who altered their schedules to be available for many of the photographs in the book. Their willingness to be involved in this project and to demonstrate different aspects of desired throwing mechanics is sincerely appreciated. Matt and Chris are two quality young men with excellent work ethic and are a credit to their parents, Randy and Vicky Ball.

I would also like to thank Bill Colman, Mike Emmert, Ed Hall and Ron Shapiro for taking the time to independently review the book and offer very constructive input. I also would like to offer a special thanks to Ron Shapiro for his efforts in attempting to attract interest in the publishing community.

Lastly, I would like to offer my thanks to the North Wake County Baseball Association. This independent, non-profit organization continues to provide an excellent opportunity for all local players to develop their abilities. It is my belief that NWCBA is one of the best independent, youth baseball programs on the East Coast.

FOREWORD

I have been pitching with the Cleveland Indians major league team for the last seven seasons. Getting to this point has not been easy. My career has been filled with highs and lows, but the one constant has been my first coach, my father.

We have been working together since I was able to throw a baseball. My father has learned about the game just as I have, but his education has been much different than mine. I think it may be easier to see what is happening while watching rather than performing. My father is an electrical engineer. He has a very different perspective on pitching mechanics than most baseball people I have met.

I have wanted to overhaul some aspect of my mechanics every off-season since I left college. My father and I sit down and discuss what my goals are for the next season and then we come up with a plan to reach those goals. The resulting change can be anything from trying to lower my time to home plate (from 2.0 seconds in 1994 to 1.3 seconds in 1995) to trying to perfect a new pitch to help get certain hitters out in 2001. No matter what the objective, though, practicing good fundamental mechanics is very important. Some of the drills in this book are big time keys to the success I have had in this game.

Sometimes I have trouble making adjustments during the season. For example, last year I was struggling coming out of spring training. It seemed that I just couldn't put the ball where I wanted. Dad watched an exhibition game where I struggled to get anyone out. During a phone call, he mentioned that my times to home were up around 1.6 seconds rather than 1.3 seconds. I listened, made a subtle change and started off the season with 10 scoreless outings, a good start to a long season. My father's eyes see and evaluate the motion of throwing a baseball and it is now instinctive for him to realize what is wrong and to be able to fix it.

He is unquestionably effective with kids in the 13-18 year old age group. It is very important that kids who want to be successful throwing a baseball learn the proper mechanics at an early age. He has managed to increase velocity in players by making adjustments in their mechanics as discussed in this book. The key to the 13-18 year old age bracket is that this group is very receptive to instruction, both mentally and physically. Older players many times have muscle memory that is very hard to break. Younger players can learn and incorporate the basics easier. For the younger player, mental focus tends to be more of a problem.

So, if you are looking for more velocity, better location and basically, nastier stuff, this is the book for you. Harnessed increased velocity and movement are qualities that any major league team will be happy to make a gamble on. Getting your foot in the door is the major stumbling block and this book will give you your best shot at getting through that door.

Listen to my old man. I did, and his words and actions have created a world in the game of baseball for me. A solid foundation and practicing the proper mechanics can get the most out of your ability.

Good luck.
Paul Shuey

INTRODUCTION

An engineering education combined with 33 years of analytical work on power electronics and communications probably seems like an unlikely background for an author of a baseball book on throwing. However, an engineering background combined with almost 50 years of baseball involvement, offers a unique set of skills that have been valuable in the analysis of the complex action of throwing a baseball.

I have written this book to help parents and coaches assist young players by improving their ability to throw a baseball. The techniques presented here are just as applicable to young women who play baseball or softball as they are to young men. The terminology in the book refers to young men, but all techniques and drills apply to both.

This book exclusively addresses the mechanics of throwing, but it is not a book just for pitchers. Instead, the instructional material that is included offers insight into the fundamentals required for all players to throw harder, with less chance of injury and with better accuracy. There is one thing everyone must realize after reading the statement about the book not being just for pitchers; if a player makes great improvement in his velocity, a future coach will probably want to see if he can pitch. A team's pitchers are generally the players that demonstrate the best velocity. There are many stories of position players that couldn't make it through the minor leagues until they switched to pitching.

Foot speed, bat speed and arm speed are the most sought after attributes of prospective baseball players at all levels of competition. These **tools** can be improved with instruction of proper technique coupled with lots of repetitions of speed drills. There is an old axiom that "you have to run fast in order to run fast." Simply stated, it means that foot speed can best be improved using speed drills as a major training component. The same thing is true for throwing. You can't expect to focus on a player's accuracy and make major improvements in his velocity. You need to focus your efforts on throwing hard if you are going to obtain improved velocity. Accuracy is something to emphasize and work on after a solid powerful throwing technique has been established as a foundation.

Over the years, I've had the benefit of working very closely with my son, Paul, as he progressed to his present status as one of the hardest throwers in the major leagues. Working with Paul has provided me with the opportunity to analyze his throwing mechanics in tremendous detail. The detailed analysis (using my engineering background) has been used to sort out the critical elements of a hard thrower's mechanics and incorporate these elements into instruction for other players.

I've also been lucky to be very involved with a strong, independent youth baseball organization (the North Wake County Baseball Association in Raleigh, North Carolina) that has provided many talented young men to work with over the years. The chance to coach and instruct good athletes at various ages has helped refine my teaching techniques. This book will hopefully provide parents, coaches and players the essential elements that will simplify throwing instruction and achieve maximum results.

Today, there are many books on the subjects of hitting and pitching and others that teach all aspects of the game of baseball. The techniques of throwing are touched upon in most, if not all of the books, but a detailed description and step by step teaching of powerful technique is generally not in texts. The same thing tends to be true of detailed analyses of poor throwing techniques and the root causes. By focusing solely on throwing, and primarily on throwing hard, the subject will be given a thorough discussion and hopefully parents and coaches will gain insight into some simple steps to make major improvements in a player's throwing ability.

This book can also be very valuable to players that are old enough to recognize the importance of improved arm speed. The instruction and drills are not too complex and a dedicated player can follow the examples in the book and execute the drills. A disciplined approach should allow the player to make significant improvement. The important point for coaches, parents and players to understand, though, is that years have gone into building the throwing mechanics that the player is presently using. For a teenage player, thousands of throws have probably been executed and all this "muscle memory" won't go away quickly. Repetition of the drills and concentration on changing old habits is needed if improvement is to be achieved.

CHAPTER 1

CHALLENGE TO PARENTS AND COACHES

Let me start by saying that my assumption is that you would like your son or daughter or all the players on your team, to have the best chance to play at the highest level of baseball competition possible. For a given player, this maximum attainable level may be all stars, high school junior varsity, varsity, college or professional. One of the most significant detriments to making any of these next levels is an inability to generate good arm speed. At every playing position on the field the ability to throw well is an advantage. Even at first base or left field, the typical positions a coach will place poor throwers, good arm speed is an asset to the team and an asset to a player who is trying to win a starting position.

It has been my experience that most young players (13-18 year olds) throw with poor technique. This statement is made after years of studying and teaching young athletes. If you read this book and find that your son is implementing a solid throwing technique, you are either a good instructor or you have been lucky to have good instructors in your youth program. Excellent technique isn't something that happens by accident and this will become more apparent as we progress through the book.

Unfortunately, a common parental response to the statement that their son's throwing technique is poor is that "my son must not be throwing with poor technique because he is successful within the league he is playing." However, statistical success for young players, especially before 14 years old, is a poor measure for a parent to utilize. The most difficult lesson, and maybe the most important lesson, for parents and coaches is that batting average, earned run average and similar performance numbers are not important for young players; **<u>tools</u>** are. **Tools**, in this discussion, means foot speed, bat speed and arm speed. (This book is specifically going to address only the **tool** of throwing but similar issues exist for the other baseball **tools**).

If you are a normal parent or coach, performance measurements <u>are</u> your yardstick for your young son's, or any individual player's,

tools. It is surprising how many times parents come to tryouts with their sons and say something like "my son will certainly make the competitive league because last season he hit.500 or had 50 strikeouts as a pitcher." These performance numbers become ingrained into parents' minds much as kids memorize their favorite professional baseball players' statistics. It's rare to hear parents describe their sons in terms of arm strength, foot speed, bat speed, etc. Of course, these measures are more difficult to quantify, but they are the true measure of where a young player ranks with his peers.

When I try a player out or evaluate him, the things that are measured are his **tools** and the techniques that are being implemented to develop these **tools**. What is the player's time in the 60? What velocity can he generate throwing the baseball? What bat speed can he generate? How quick are his feet? Then, I attempt to associate a different set of questions to the player. What is his running form? Is he using his whole body in the throwing technique? Similarly, is he using good fundamentals in his hitting technique?

Evaluations of tools and associated techniques are used in place of last season's performance numbers for any player I evaluate up until he is well into his college career. **Tools** determine <u>potential</u> for improvement in performance.

If you ever watch a good professional baseball scout working to analyze a prospect, you will notice him moving from one side of the field to the other as well as behind home plate. The scout is trying to determine how good the player's tools and techniques are. This information tells the scout a lot about a player's risk of injury as well as his "upside potential." A scout may actually be more excited about a player with poor technique that throws 85 MPH than he is about a polished player with great technique throwing the same velocity. The scout may feel that with good instruction in the team's minor league system, the player with poor technique may be able to make more progress (especially if he projects the player to be bigger and stronger).

A professional scout will evaluate a player's hitting, hitting with power, running speed, throwing and fielding. He makes an assessment of these current **tools** and tries to project a player's God given physical abilities into future **tools**. The scout's evaluation generates an overall rating that relates the player's projected tools to the average major league baseball player.

For the majority of physically average young players who demonstrate poor throwing technique, the baseball experience is limited to a recreational activity unless they develop some other aspect of the game to a very high level. For the players with poor throwing technique and correspondingly poor velocity, their team assignments from tryouts are normally not to the competitive or travel leagues. End of the season all-star team selection typically doesn't happen. While the game of baseball is still a lot of fun, the same players could achieve a higher level of enjoyment if they developed good throwing technique at a young age.

Quite a few players below the age of 14 generate good performance numbers even though they demonstrate poor throwing, running or hitting technique. These players many times have overcome poor technique because of their comparative large size or strength. These physical factors can postpone inevitable failures that result when players with proper technique start to catch up physically. A large dose of failure can be very depressing for the young player who has always been successful growing up. I've seen many young guys just drop out of baseball when they see themselves becoming average or below average players and quit making post season teams. The age of 14 is mentioned because this is the age when most young men begin a significant growth spurt. From this age forward, there is typically less size and strength differentiation among most players.

Even at the age of 20 years old, though, some college and minor league players exhibit poor technique with some of their tools. As mentioned before, the player may have developed another aspect of the game to a very high level or his enormous physical gifts are allowing him to achieve above average performance numbers. If these outstanding athletes are subjected to quality instruction, and have the discipline to work on their weaknesses, they can incorporate better technique and their **tools** can be improved.

After a player is about 15 years old, however, he may have as much as 10 years experience throwing incorrectly. From this age forward, it is not an easy task to change a player's throwing technique. A large number of repetitions are needed to overcome the muscle memory from years of incorrect technique. A dedicated work effort is required, even for the most gifted athletes.

CHAPTER 2

PROBLEMS RELATED TO POOR TECHNIQUE

Poor throwing technique typically causes one or more of the following three problems.

- The player doesn't achieve the maximum velocity that is possible <u>for him</u>.
- Stress is placed on the throwing elbow or shoulder and soreness or injury occurs.
- The player's throwing accuracy is not optimal <u>for him</u>.

I've underlined <u>for him</u> because two players with excellent technique won't necessarily generate the same arm speed or accuracy. Hopefully, both will reduce the chance for injury. God given body makeup differentiates players' maximum tools. Unfortunately, all players with excellent technique just will not be able to throw 100 miles per hour.

Velocity

It was mentioned earlier that arm speed is one of the most important TOOLS for a baseball player. The majority of the emphasis and suggested techniques in this book are offered to achieve greater arm speed and therefore higher velocity of the thrown ball.

Coaches have a tendency to compare one player against another, but proper instruction needs to focus on maximizing a player's individual skill. This is a difficult problem because as you try to establish an absolute measure, it is difficult not to use teammates as the reference. When I work with young players, I first evaluate their technique and try to determine how close to optimal they are. After making this subjective evaluation, I think in terms of making 5 or 10% improvement in their velocity through improved technique (unrelated to any other player's ability.) If a coordinated, strong 16-year-old player is throwing 75 MPH with poor technique and you tell him there might be 10% more velocity available, the player tends to be motivated to work toward the achievable goal.

However, if you establish a goal of getting to where he is throwing Major League average (85+ MPH), the player will be excited at first, but when progress is slow the goal will seem too far away to be achievable. The advantage of an incremental goal for the individual is that when the player goes from 75MPH to 78MPH he has achieved a significant portion of the goal that was originally established. Using that positive feedback he feels he is making progress, and he is. Progress is necessary to keep a player working on changing tendencies that have been ingrained over many years. It simply isn't reasonable to expect a 16-year-old player to increase his velocity 10% within a couple months of making significant technical changes.

Injury

When I begin to analyze a young player who exhibits poor technique I generally can tell if he has had previous arm or shoulder pain. Poor throwing technique that can cause injury only takes a few different forms, and usually the result is that the arm gets into a "weak" throwing position. The result of a weak throwing position is that the small muscles and tendons of the shoulder and elbow carry too much of the load in comparison to the major muscles of the lower body, trunk and back.

Injury from poor throwing technique is very similar in concept to a weight lifter that hurts his lower back performing the bench press. The injury may not strictly be from trying to lift too much weight, but rather, from the added weight creating poor technique that forces his back to arch abnormally. With proper bench technique the lower back stays in solid, straight alignment contacting the bench, and the intended upper body muscle groups carry the load.

With a throwing athlete, there are key points in the delivery that must be correct to allow the athlete to achieve a "strong" throwing position and a much better chance of long term, injury free competition. In general, <u>any elbow or shoulder pain in the throwing athlete is an indication of a technique problem and the player should not be allowed to continue throwing with pain</u>. Continued pain in muscles and tendons will cause atrophy and long term harm. A "no pain, no gain" philosophy for the throwing athlete makes "no sense."

Over the years, I've found most baseball people to be very "old school" with regard to throwing mechanics. Many times, instructors teach the things that worked for them. Other times, instructors do not want to change a player's mechanics for fear of causing injury. There tends to be a significant difference in the approach to instruction of throwers in comparison to the approach to instruction of hitters. Almost every hitting instructor has a set of "absolutes" that they emphasize and they have little concern about implementing these absolutes with all the players that come to them for instruction.

In contrast, most pitching instructors treat a player's throwing mechanics as though they were personal. In other words, each player supposedly has a set of throwing mechanics that are appropriate for the player's particular body style or build. Contrary to this view, I think most players simply get started throwing incorrectly because proper instruction isn't available until techniques are ingrained. The older the player is when changes are taught, the more difficult the task is to implement the changes. It is simply easier to slightly modify techniques than to overhaul them. As a result, most players are taught to make the best of the throwing methods that have taken them to where they are.

A player's age and work ethic determines the success that can be achieved by making major changes in mechanics to reduce the chance of injury. The older the player, the more muscle memory he has to overcome and the more repetitions it will take to make the required changes. In addition, for older players there is some risk that short-term soreness can develop from a new set of throwing mechanics. This may be because a different arm action results in a new muscle group being utilized or simply because new methods take a player that was throwing 75 MPH and get him to throwing 80 MPH. In this latter case, the player will be putting his shoulder and elbow through more range of motion than he was previously and some soreness may develop. One of the first things I ask a new student to do is incorporate a daily rotator cuff strengthening program. In this manner, if we are successful in increasing velocity, the muscles and tendons will be strengthened to take the increased load.

7

Accuracy

The third problem associated with poor throwing technique is inaccuracy. Bad techniques can cause inaccuracy, but an accurate thrower doesn't necessarily possess good technique. Good accuracy is simply the result of a repeatable method by a good athlete. An average player can be extremely accurate using a dart thrower's technique if it is repeated consistently. By contrast, outstanding athletes like Cal Ripken, Nomar Garciaparro and Kevin Brown can throw the ball accurately from many different angles, using many different throwing techniques. The throwing technique that is the subject of this book is intended to achieve both powerful and accurate throws even if you are not an outstanding athlete.

Accuracy is the last of the three problems listed in this segment of the book. This clarification is made to emphasize that young players should not have a primary focus on accuracy. I know this is a terrible concept for most youth coaches, because the team can't win if the players aren't throwing accurately. However, the whole concept of player development reduces the emphasis on performance and winning games and increases the emphasis on improvement in TOOLS.

Young players should be encouraged to throw hard at every opportunity (using proper technique), rather than focusing on accuracy. This is one lesson I learned from working with my son Paul. As he was growing up, it's hard to recall a time that he ever threw easier trying to be more accurate. By consistently throwing hard as he grew up, near maximal effort became normal effort. His accuracy was not always good as a young player, but it continually improved with each season he played. Today, Paul still isn't considered to be an outstanding control pitcher, but the combination of explosive stuff and better than average major league command makes him one of the most dominant relief pitchers in the game.

A good example of focusing on accuracy to the detriment of powerful technique occurred one fall in a baseball camp for 14 and under players. A lot of time was spent in one session working on proper throwing technique. The camp director finished a one-hour training session with a game where the players split into pairs. Each player dropped his cap down beside him as a throwing target for his partner. The winners of the game were to be the quickest pair of players to throw and hit the partner's hat 5 times. The winners would get a few baseball cards as their prize. Every player in camp immediately resorted to a throwing technique that simulated a game of darts, as discussed earlier. Not one element of the proper technique that they had worked on for more than an hour was being used in this accuracy drill.

So, to summarize this section, the main point of emphasis is that it is critical to develop a young player's arm speed through development of proper technique, and parents need to de-emphasize the young player's performance numbers. If your son is throwing harder without any shoulder or elbow pain, but occasionally making inaccurate throws, continue to congratulate him on his arm speed improvement rather than chastising him for throwing errors. After the proper mechanics have been repeated over and over, they will become more natural to the player. As the mechanics become repeatable, the player should be able to throw the baseball with good velocity using the same release point and his accuracy should improve.

CHAPTER 3

TEACHING YOURSELF TO SEE

To reiterate, this book is mainly intended for coaches and parents that want to help improve their player's throwing ability. One of the most important things that you, as a coach, need to do is train yourself to see what is happening in the middle of a fast moving, complex set of movements. My guess is that now when you watch a player throw, you see the overall action and have a lot of difficulty being certain what the causes are for problems the player may be having. Typically, the things that are seen the best are the slowest moving parts which occur at the beginning and the end of the throwing action.

As we proceed through the following examples and pictures that demonstrate excellent technique, we will see the results of a 35-millimeter camera catching the fast moving throwing action at various points. A good quality 35-millimeter camera and an experienced photographer can stop the desired throwing elements in action. A video camera allows the complete sequence of throwing events to be captured and a high quality VCR with "jog shuttle" capability allows each frame to be viewed for analysis of technique. These state of the art pieces of electronic equipment are extremely valuable when you are trying to understand a player's mechanics in order to provide good instruction.

However, you won't have a still camera or a video camera with you most of the time, so you need to teach yourself to visualize your players much the same way a camera does. When I watch a player, it takes several throws to get a complete understanding of his mechanics. With each throw, I force my mind to focus only on one aspect of the action. Effectively, I take "a snapshot" of one specific point out of the complete motion during each throw. Then, I try to mentally tie the individual "frames" together. Using this method, I can determine where most problem areas exist and how the overall action is tied together. The camera technique is not simple, and requires time to master, but it is the only method that will allow you to dissect a complex set of movements when you don't have your camera available. After working on this framing technique at several practices, you should be able to begin to isolate what is going on with the critical parts of a player's throwing motion.

The best practice technique for "training yourself to see" is to focus on one point in a player's throwing motion over and over until you know exactly what the body components are doing. For example, let's assume you are going to view the player at "launch" (the following picture of Paul shows him just as his front foot touches the ground.) You will need to focus on exactly how the throwing hand is positioned, how high the elbow is relative to the shoulder, how the weight is distributed (heels or balls of the feet, lead leg or back leg) and how the body is positioned (closed or open). Each of these aspects of the "launch" position takes multiple throws to obtain multiple mental frames. As you are first learning this visualization technique you may need to view the player from several different angles in order to get a complete picture. As you gain experience, you will find keys that will allow you to limit the number of angles and the number of throws that you require to "see" a player's technique.

Let me finish by saying that, while it's very beneficial to work on the framing techniques described here, I still utilize a video camera whenever possible. This piece of equipment, coupled with a high quality VCR, develops a very fine resolution of the complex and fast moving actions of throwing a baseball.

I've found that when you use the video camera and spend time with the player to go over the tape, elements you are trying to teach begin to make more sense. In most cases, before seeing the videotape the player thinks he is doing something completely different than what the tape shows. A typical example is the case where the player thinks he is throwing from a high arm angle (overhand slot) and the reality may be much closer to sidearm. There many other examples where the player can benefit by viewing the tape and listening to instruction simultaneously.

Normally, as Paul is finishing his off-season conditioning and throwing and is approaching his game velocity, we take the video camera and review all aspects of his throwing mechanics. Before he gets too far into spring training, I request a tape of one of his outings to again review his mechanics in detail. The review is used to evaluate any areas that could subject Paul to potential problems. After spring training, I try to videotape (off satellite) as many outings as possible during the season, continually reviewing the tapes in slow motion, looking for mechanical problems as well as attempting to review the many other aspects of the art of pitching.

When you have achieved a good understanding of the "absolutes" in this book and have reviewed the various stop action pictures throughout the book, you'll hopefully understand the critical aspects of throwing that you need to train your mind to capture.

CHAPTER 4

IT ALL STARTS WRONG

Well, maybe at this point you are questioning whether your young player is throwing with optimal technique or not. Let's begin by analyzing why your son might not be throwing with the best technique.

When I hand my four year old granddaughter, Morgan, a ball and ask her to throw it to me; she takes the ball palm up (the easiest way she can hold it), faces me and throws the ball using only the throwing hand, forearm, upper arm and shoulder joint. The elbow leads the action and the throw is a push, much like a shot putter's release. There is no involvement of the lower body in this throwing motion as the following picture shows.

If no one does any substantial throwing instruction between now and when Morgan is 10 years old, she likely will be throwing in a very similar manner at that age. Actually, when I go to junior league tryouts in the spring it isn't uncommon to see a few 13 year old players, with limited playing experience, using throwing techniques similar to Morgan.

It needs to be stated here that there isn't anything that prevents girls from throwing with optimal technique. Rather, bad throwing technique for girls occurs because the majority of young women do not grow up competing in youth baseball or softball programs where proper instruction is offered. As stated earlier, if a young player does not receive proper instruction he is almost certain to have bad throwing habits later in life.

Both of my sons attended the University of North Carolina on baseball scholarships. Being around UNC's Boshamer Stadium on a regular basis provided me an opportunity to meet several of the young women that played on the UNC softball team. Most of the members of the women's team are exceptional female athletes that have focused on their sport and have received good instruction growing up. Good instruction, provided at a young age and coupled with lots of drill repetitions, has allowed most of these women the opportunity to throw with excellent technique.

Since the statement has been made that young kids start throwing with poor technique, how do we determine what good technique is? Well, the most obvious answer is that the hardest throwers in the major leagues probably are utilizing close to optimal technique. To understand optimal technique, then, we need to break down the step by step throwing method employed by these players. (Even though this book is only going to utilize one major leaguer for illustration, the author has videotaped and studied hundreds of major league players to determine that the techniques presented here are characteristic of the majority of major league players who generate maximum velocity.)

Paul Shuey, my older son, has been clocked at 100 mph on a few occasions in the big leagues. He is generally classified as having one of the "best arms" on the Cleveland Indians staff as well as in the major leagues. I have put the term "best arms" in quotes, because I believe the term is a misnomer. It is my assertion that a "great arm" requires great technique that utilizes a tremendously strong and quick lower body. Players with "great arms" are blessed with outstanding shoulder flexibility and fast twitch arm muscles, but the ability to generate rotational energy in the lower half of the body and then translate that energy from the lower half to the upper half really determines the "great arm." All truly hard throwers possess extremely powerful legs and midsections and utilize these major muscle groups to the maximum when they accelerate the baseball.

We will begin to analyze Paul's throwing mechanics in detail and in doing so attempt to outline the critical aspects of a powerful throwing technique. As we analyze throwing mechanics it's important to again emphasize that these mechanics need not be thought of exclusively as pitching mechanics. An optimal throwing technique is just as applicable to an outfielder, an infielder or a catcher as it is to a pitcher.

CHAPTER 5

GETTING THE UPPER BODY READY

The detailed discussion of optimal throwing mechanics is going to be segmented so that the upper body actions and lower body actions are isolated. In addition, the discussion and teaching concepts will break the mechanics into the movements prior to "launch" and after "launch." "Launch," as shown in the previous picture of Paul in Chapter 3, is the key throwing position because it is the point where the throwing action should switch from the reverse (backward) arm swing to the forward arm whip. It is important to emphasize that this book is intended to guide players in the establishment of an optimal "launch" position from which a powerful turn can be executed to generate maximum arm speed.

One characteristic of throwing mechanics that will not generate maximum velocity is the lack of a defined launch position. This type of throwing motion is typical for the majority of young players and is best understood by stating that the throwing action blends together smoothly and energy is expended almost linearly over the whole process. This throwing method is compared to a hard thrower's mechanics that achieve a defined launch position; from which energy is developed almost instantaneously. A smooth throwing action is even typical of many advanced players that I see in high school, in college and in the professional ranks. A smooth, even transition from the reverse action through the forward action can be accurate and can prevent injury, but it cannot generate maximum velocity. Maximum velocity occurs when there is a violent, maximum effort turn that is executed, starting from the ideal launch position.

You may be asking yourself, "why, if some professional players throw with a blended technique, is it so important that young players learn to throw with the techniques in this book." The answer is that major league players typically have exceptional, if not freak of nature, athletic ability and physical gifts. The fact that a six foot six, 240 pound major league pitcher can throw 90 plus miles per hour with a less than optimal set of mechanics doesn't mean that a five foot eleven, 175 pound high school player will get anywhere close to that velocity using the same technique. The average player with average athletic ability must utilize every bit of leverage and technique available to him to get close to the average major league arm speed.

So, the intent of this book is to break the mechanics down into the fewest number of steps that will allow the player to get into the ideal launch position, accelerate the arm to the maximum amount and then allow the arm to decelerate through a controlled finish. We will begin by working on the critical upper body actions.

The Grip

One significant problem that reduces velocity for a lot of young players is the actual hand position on the baseball, and this problem is caused by the player wanting, subconsciously, to be in control of the ball. I believe the problem arises at a young age, when the player needs to grip the ball tightly to hold it in his small hand. The typical poor grip consists of the ball tucked deep in the hand so that all of the joints of the middle and index fingers make solid contact. The incorrect grip for the thumb is with the soft pad, opposite the thumbnail, in full contact with the <u>side</u> of the ball. Using this grip, the player feels like he has complete control of the ball, and he does. Paul attempts to show this incorrect grip in the following picture.

One of the most obvious results of this strong, controlling grip on the ball is a resultant ball flight that isn't true and straight to the target. Rather, the thrown ball has side spin and the flight of the ball tends to curve and sink. This lack of "carry" on the baseball is most obvious when you ask players to throw to you from the outfield. The increased throwing distance allows more time to view the path of the ball (another aspect of teaching yourself to see.) Typically, a young player's grip pressure will be quite high and this further causes a weak ball flight.

What the coach and player need to understand is that a proper grip isn't the controlling grip just described. The proper grip needs to allow the maximum whip of the ball through relaxation in the arm and hand. As a coach, you need to evaluate your player's hand size and determine how closely the player can come to achieving the optimal grip. In general, the younger the player the more difficult it will be to exactly implement the proper grip.

The ideal grip for all players depends on a relaxed hand and wrist. The index and middle finger should make contact with the ball with light pressure applied primarily from the surface beyond the first knuckle. The feel is that the ball is out on the tips of the fingers. The thumb should be on the opposite side of the ball from a point that is centered between the fingers—if the fingers are on top; the thumb should be on the bottom. The edge of the thumb should contact the ball, near the side of the thumbnail. There should be sufficient room between the ball and the palm of the hand to insert two fingers. In the following picture, Paul shows his natural grip that implements the above goals. Again, the player's age and physical size will determine the amount of spacing that can be achieved. The ring finger and little finger should be essentially off the ball, only making incidental contact.

After a young player has thrown with a firm, controlling grip for several years, the optimal grip will feel very weak and uncomfortable.

19

I generally ask the player to practice working with the ball independent of throwing, trying to make the correct grip feel more comfortable. Unfortunately, the player will generally resort to the old comfortable grip when he starts to throw. The ideal grip takes a lot of repetitions before there is a change in what feels natural. There is a grip drill in the back of the book that should help, if it is repeated many times.

ABSOLUTE # 1

A proper grip uses light pressure of two fingertips on top of the ball and the edge of the thumb on the bottom…

One of the points emphasized in the grip drill in the back of the book is the importance of achieving the four-seam grip as shown in the adjoining picture. The term "four seams" means that when the ball is thrown, it will have backspin imparted that forces four different seam segments to cut sequentially through the air. This throwing grip, shown below for a left-handed thrower, achieves the highest average velocity. For example, there may be as much as 3 to 4 miles per hour difference in the average velocity of a pitch thrown using a four-seam grip compared to a pitch thrown using a two-seam grip. This is true even though the velocity of the ball coming out of the hand is the same for both grips (A Jugs gun generally measures maximum velocity out of the hand and a Ray gun generally measures average velocity.) In addition to more average velocity, the ball will tend to stay straighter when thrown with a four-seam grip. Both of these facts are important to all position players.

A Good Start

Now that the correct grip has been established, the next step in understanding good throwing technique is to develop the correct start to the arm action. The following two pictures of Paul provide demonstrations of the arm action just after beginning the throwing motion. Paul's body is square to the target (lead shoulder pointed to the plate) and the ball is in the throwing hand, palm down. Careful attention to these two pictures will find Paul's non-throwing hand (glove hand) also beginning palm down. The throwing arm is nearly at full extension as it moves though a relaxed, continuous swing, headed to a point where the elbow is above the shoulder.

It needs to be pointed out, in reference to these starting photos, that most of the problems that players have at the release point or afterwards are a result of starting wrong or going wrong early in the throwing motion. <u>If you, as the coach or the player, aren't going to fix the problems at the start of the throwing motion, you shouldn't try to fix the problems at the finish</u>.

ABSOLUTE # 2

Hands break with palms directed downward (throwing hand on top of the ball)...

In addition to the two previous pictures of Paul, the following two pictures show how Matt and Chris Ball implement the same starting positions with the throwing hand and the glove hand. Matt and Chris are strong, twin brothers that play in the North Wake County Baseball Association. Matt is left-handed and Chris is right-handed.

Both players demonstrate the throwing hand on top of the baseball as it separates from the glove thumbs down to start the motion. Much like the previous two pictures of Paul, these two shots of Matt and Chris also show that the glove hand should also start palm down. Both players are set up with their body square to the target in these still pictures, but the focus here is exclusively on the smooth swing of the arms. The lower body will be analyzed later in the book.

For the majority of young players, the ball gets on top of the throwing hand at the beginning of the arm swing and the final result is a weak throwing technique. Again, the early position that the player achieves with the throwing hand and glove hand determines the player's ability to achieve a strong position later in the throwing motion.

The next two pictures show Paul's arm action slightly later in the throwing motion. These pictures show the continuation of a smooth swing of the throwing arm and lead arm. The throwing hand is on top of the ball at all times and the lead shoulder moves in line with or slightly closed to the target. (The term closed means that Paul's back is turned to the plate rather than his chest being turned to the plate.)

The smooth, relaxed arm swing cannot be overemphasized to young players. Generally, players rush through this part of the action with tight arm muscles, and the result is that the ball is primarily thrown using the energy developed by the arm rather than by the largest muscles in the lower half and mid-section of the body.

Proper throwing instruction should focus on insuring that the reverse arm swing always gets the arm up to where the elbow is even or above the shoulder prior to initiating a strong turning action of the lower and upper body. This ideal launch position for the arm is shown in the above picture of Paul. In this ideal position, the hand is still on top of the ball with the palm of the hand pointed back toward second base.

Later in the book, we will discuss how position players, as well as pitchers, can achieve this same ideal launch position for the throwing side and the glove side. For now, though, the important thing to fully understand is how the ideal arm swing and ideal launch position are achieved.

At the point in the throwing motion where the arms are approximately horizontal, camera angles have been added to address the third critical element of good throwing technique.

The following three pictures of Paul, Matt and Chris are taken prior to the launch position and are taken with the camera aligned parallel with the shoulder blades. The point to emphasize here is that the throwing arm does not swing behind the shoulder blades. In the picture of Paul, even though his upper body is very closed (again, Paul's back is pointed more to home plate than his chest), the camera clearly shows that his throwing arm and lead arm are in line with his shoulders.

For the two pictures of Matt and Chris, the camera is situated behind the players, directly in line with the target. Both players show that the arm swing has achieved an arm position that is in line with the shoulders and the target. This is the ideal early arm position that will allow the achievement of a strong position at launch. The reverse arm swing has not gone behind the back at any point, and in addition, the reverse arm swing has maintained the hand on top of the baseball throughout. These essential points, coupled with the proper grip that was described earlier, define the critical elements of the arm and hand motion prior to initiating the actions that will actually accelerate the ball towards the target.

ABSOLUTE # 3

The reverse arm swing should not go behind the back at any point…

It was mentioned earlier that it can be a good teaching aid to think about the throwing motion as consisting of two parts. The first part involves the reverse arm swing where the player works to achieve the ideal "launch" position. Until "launch" is achieved, the arm is going away from the intended target. After "launch" the arm is being accelerated toward the target. The next two pictures show Matt and Chris in the launch position.

If the player's arm gets to a strong position at "launch" he is ready for the lower body to accelerate the arm. A strong position at launch has the ball pointed backward with the elbow above the shoulder. Please study all of these upper body pictures in this chapter leading up to and including "launch," because we will reference these correct positions throughout the rest of the book.

Proper Arm Swing

In order for you to really grasp the "behind the back" problem mentioned earlier, I'm going to ask you to actually go through correct and incorrect arm swings. First, stand with your feet and chest facing a wall about a foot away. Start with a ball in your throwing hand, held palm down at your leg, and slowly swing your arm at full extension, parallel to the wall. Take your arm up to the point where your elbow is well above the shoulder and the palm of the hand is pointed away from your head. You should be able to execute this reverse arm swing with no discomfort or tightness in the shoulder. The hand should stay the same distance from the wall from start to finish of the reverse swing.

Improper Arm Swing

Behind the Back

Now, return your hand and the ball to the starting position next to your leg and again slowly swing your arm palm down, except this time take your arm behind your back (the throwing hand moves away from the wall) as you swing to the rear. You will reach a point in the reverse arm swing where you no longer can continue an upward motion if the palm continues to point down. There is a restriction (impingement) generated within the shoulder socket that limits the height of the arm swing (as the following two pictures of Matt and Chris attempt to demonstrate.)

If you get into this improper position and are going to get your arm to continue upward to where the elbow is above the shoulder, you must rotate your hand so the palm is pointed upwards (hand under the ball.) This movement relieves the pressure in the shoulder socket, allowing you to continue the arm swing to get your elbow above the shoulder; but now the ball will be pointed toward your head. The following two pictures of Matt and Chris show this improper technique that takes the reverse swing behind the back and is compensated for by rotating the hand to the "palm under" position.

If your arm swing doesn't allow the ball to be pointed away from your head, you will be in a weak throwing position and an optimal turning motion will not be achievable. Many young players develop a sidearm throwing motion because of this behind the back problem. Others develop the throwing technique that we have discussed previously where the weight drifts to the front side, the lead hip and shoulder open early and the throwing motion becomes a smooth, linear process that doesn't achieve maximum velocity.

One major factor that contributes to this "behind the back" problem is a fast reverse swing. When a player slings his arm to the rear, there is a tendency for the arm to not stay parallel to the shoulders. The most significant cause of a fast reverse swing is a late separation of the hands as the throwing motion starts. In other words, the player keeps the ball in the glove too long.

If you remember, in the very first part of the book the comment was made that you need to fix the problems with the beginning of the motion. If you are not going to fix these starting problems, you won't be able to resolve the problems at the finish. The throwing mechanics are complex enough when the player starts properly. When he starts incorrectly, the mechanics get more and more complex to compensate for weak positions of the arm. Again, great athletes may be able to make these adjustments, but average players need to do all the basics properly.

One key concept to get across to young players is *that you can't get your arm up into the ideal "launch" position too early: you can only get there too late.* I normally will overemphasize this point by just standing with the throwing arm in the ideal launch position (elbow above the shoulder, ball pointed back) to begin the rest of the throwing motion. The player sees that the same throwing action can result without all the motion that leads up to the ideal launch position.

I'll add here that overemphasis or exaggeration of technique is something I use a lot to get a point across. If a player throws sidearm, I'll try to get him straight overhand in drills to hope the result will be a compromise, three quarter release point. Similar over-compensation concepts are used for other points in the throwing mechanics.

To continue, the emphasis should always be to get the player's hands separated early (ball out of the glove) to start the arm action early. This early separation will allow the arm to get up in position early, without a fast arm swing. The key checkpoint is that the elbow and the ball should be above the shoulder before the front foot touches the ground. (You need to understand that we haven't begun to discuss the lower body mechanics yet.)

Having the elbow and ball above the shoulder early will help to guarantee that no turning action is initiated to move the arm forward to the target without the arm in a good, strong position. Most players keep their hands together (ball in the glove) too long and as a result, do not have enough time to make a relaxed smooth reverse swing to the proper "launch" position. The faster the player slings his arm to the rear, the less relaxed his arm action is and the more chance there is that the ideal position will not be consistently achieved.

It has been stated several times that a strong "launch" position with the palm (ball) pointed to the rear and elbow above the shoulder can't be achieved if the arm swing goes behind the back very far. This is one of the most common mistakes young players make and one that needs to be corrected at as early an age as possible. (Refer to the wall drill in the back of the book for one of the best ways to correct this problem.)

Stopping the Reverse Swing

Another common problem players have is stopping the reverse arm action. They typically start correctly and then stop the reverse swing before the elbow gets above the shoulder. I've heard some coaches refer to this problem as "sticking". A good athlete will "feel" this very weak position of the elbow below the shoulder and will compensate by drifting his weight forward to the front leg to allow his arm to finally get up into a stronger position. This forward weight shift is the most significant characteristic of the blended throwing technique that was mentioned earlier in the book. (We are beginning to touch onto the lower body discussion, but it is important to understand that an incorrect start will significantly impede the player's ability to generate maximum velocity.)

The end result of a discontinuous reverse arm swing is a non-optimal launch position with the majority of the player's weight moved to the front leg which makes explosive rotation around the spine very difficult. The result of decreased rotational energy is less than maximum velocity. As discussed earlier, great athletes can throw successfully with a blended overall technique and be successful, but average athletes will be more subject to injury and mediocre velocity. The average athlete needs to do everything as close to perfect as possible in order to generate above average velocity and stay injury free.

Again, to emphasize, the pictures of Paul, Matt and Chris demonstrate that the recommended throwing position at "launch" has the palm pointing to the rear and the elbow above the shoulder. If you can get a young player to achieve this position, he will be a long way toward achieving optimal throwing results.

Elbow Below the Shoulder

Having the throwing elbow below shoulder level is described as a "weak" throwing position throughout this book. In order for you to better understand this, I'll again ask you to do a simple experiment before we proceed.

First, lay flat on your back on the floor with your throwing arm extended to the side. Bend your elbow at a right angle and position the palm of your hand so that it is facing the ceiling. If you have your elbow in a position even or slightly above shoulder level and you relax your arm, you will find the back of your hand and the lower part of the back of your forearm touch the floor comfortably.

Now, if you lower the elbow 6 or 8 inches below shoulder level and keep the elbow at a right angle, you will notice the hand and lower part of the forearm come off the floor due to restriction in the shoulder. In other words, there is less flexibility to allow reverse rotation in the shoulder socket when the elbow is below the shoulder. When you move your elbow back even with or above your shoulder the hand and forearm will again touch the floor comfortably. Repeat this exercise a few times to gain a clear understanding of how having the elbow below the shoulder restricts the reverse rotation capability of the arm in the shoulder socket.

This simple experiment provides you with insight into the need to have a player's elbow above his shoulder prior to initiating the acceleration phase of the throwing action. You certainly want as little restriction as possible in the shoulder joint to reduce the chance of injury. If you look at any hard thrower when his arm is in the fully flexed position (reverse rotated in the shoulder socket), you get an appreciation for the need to minimize restriction in the shoulder socket area. We will discuss the need for reverse shoulder socket rotation when the lower body components of a maximum effort throwing motion are covered.

ABSOLUTE # 4

The elbow should be above the shoulder and the palm pointed backward at the "launch" position...

Relaxation

A point that hasn't been emphasized yet is the need for the arm, wrist and hand to be relaxed up to and through launch. If you will think about the term "whip," you will envision a leather strap that you swing to maximize the resultant speed of the tip. With a bullwhip, the tip can actually exceed the speed of sound with maximum whip action. While I don't think the hand can be accelerated sufficiently to break the sound barrier, I would like the coach and player to think of the arm action in much the same way as we do a whip. If the arm is loose and relaxed up to and through launch, the lower body can generate an explosive rotation that will maximize the speed of the hand (the equivalent of the end of the whip.)

If the arm is held tightly by the muscles the player will not transfer the maximum energy from the lower body to the arm. Arm speed will not be optimal. When a player achieves a relaxed arm position prior to the lower body and upper body executing a turn, a full flex of the arm in the shoulder socket results as shown in the following picture of Paul. Extremely good flexibility in the shoulder allows the maximum amount of whip of the arm and ball to occur. Notice in the picture that the elbow is even or slightly above the shoulder.

This is really the essential component of a hard thrower's technique and the most important concept for coaches and players to understand. A hard turning action of the lower body, upper body and trunk loads energy into the shoulder socket, much like winding a spring. As the above picture shows, Paul has completed his hard turn and his throwing arm is fully reverse rotated in the shoulder socket. (The spring is wound as tightly as possible.)

For young players, a relaxed arm and a relaxed grip on the ball are definitely not comfortable concepts. They want to be in control of the ball as we have discussed previously, and they have a definite tendency to "muscle" the ball with their arm and hand. They have thrown using this method for a long time and this is the technique that is comfortable.

When the arm is tight as the player starts the throwing action, a fluid reverse arm swing doesn't occur. Instead, the reverse arm swing has excessive bend at the elbow and the arm movement has a tendency to be restricted. The result of any restriction in the reverse arm swing is a poor position at launch that causes a push of the baseball rather than a whip of the baseball. A restricted pushing motion generates much less velocity than can be achieved with a relaxed arm that is whipped by the strongest muscles of the body. As a coach, you want to get the player to have a very relaxed set of muscles in the lower and upper arm prior to and at the launch position. In all sports, relaxed muscles are fast muscles and this is also true in throwing.

ABSOLUTE # 5

The arm, wrist and shoulder needs to be relaxed if the ball is to be "whipped" by the lower body rotation...

There is a weighted ball drill in the back of the book that emphasizes a relaxed arm and allows the player to feel the reverse rotation in the shoulder socket.

As a relaxation test, when the player takes the ball back toward the launch position you should be able to pop the back of his hand firmly and have the ball drop free. Occasionally, when I'm throwing batting practice I'll actually have the ball fall out of my hand during the backward swing. That is the type of relaxation that allows maximum whip of the wrist, forearm, elbow and upper arm. The powerful throwing concept being taught in this book emphasizes relaxation of the hand and arm.

CHAPTER 6

THROWING WITH YOUR LEGS

Up to this point, we have almost exclusively discussed the positions of the arms and hands in developing proper throwing technique. The reason for this emphasis is the idea that if the throwing arm doesn't get into a strong position the player will not be able to use the lower body and trunk to accelerate the arm to achieve maximum velocity. As was stated earlier, if you don't fix the start of the mechanics, you won't be able to fix the finish. In addition, if you don't get the arm action optimized you can't really focus on the lower body and trunk for rotation. I'll try to explain this in more detail.

The goal of establishing good arm action is to be in a position to utilize the major muscle groups of the body to throw the baseball. If the coach, parent or player understands how to achieve the five absolutes related to the arm and hand that have been discussed so far, he is ready to get the lower portion of the body and the trunk involved. As has been clearly stated, this level of achievement in perfecting the arm action is a lot to ask and many repetitions of new drills will be required. However, if the ideal arm action and ideal launch position are achieved, the lower body and trunk can execute a hard rotation around the spine that will whip the throwing arm and hand. Without achieving a good arm position, a sub-optimal lower body and/or upper body turning action will be executed.

Good Feet

First, it needs to be noted here that there are always plays in the game of baseball that require the player to make throws without being able to establish the ideal launch position. This book will not address the various techniques for accomplishing athletic throws on the run, unbalanced throws as part of double play pivots or throws made with the player's momentum going away from the target. Rather, this discussion will focus on getting the player's lower body into position for optimal velocity generation. The majority of all plays can be executed using the techniques outlined throughout this book if a player develops good, quick feet.

An infielder, outfielder or catcher may have a different starting position for each throw that is to be accomplished. These various starting positions require the position player to have good, quick feet in order to get into the desired launch position for each throw. The start of any lower body action to prepare to throw the baseball needs to establish the back foot square, or at a right angle, to the target. This proper starting position is shown in the last two pictures, of the following set of three. Chris needed quick feet to get into the solid fielding position exhibited in the first of the three pictures and continued to utilize quickness to achieve the simple jab step that squared his upper body to the target and began the action of squaring the lower body.

ABSOLUTE # 6

The pivot foot needs to be square to the target until launch…

For a pitcher, this square position is almost forced because he has the pitching rubber to use for the alignment of his pivot foot. For position players, there isn't a similar alignment mechanism. For most position players, getting the back foot square to the target is something that must be emphasized all the time. During throwing drills every day, each position player should establish his pivot foot along the foul line, or a similarly drawn line, when throwing to a partner. Players should also be expected to execute the proper jab step every time they achieve a controlled fielding position from which they will throw the ball.

When an infielder or catcher is in a dynamic mode, responding to a pitch or fielding a ground ball, his first action after catching the baseball is to take a short jab step <u>in front.</u> This jab step squares the pivot foot (back foot) to the target and begins some momentum toward the target. The next movement of the lower body is to take <u>the heel</u> of the lead foot toward the target. These two simple movements are made with the weight on the balls of the feet. When the ball of the front foot lands, the throwing elbow should be above the shoulder with the ball pointed away from the target as discussed earlier in the text. In this ideal launch position, significantly more weight should be on the back foot than on the front foot.

The preceding three pictures of Chris Ball demonstrate the position player's required technique if he is to be in position to generate maximum velocity throwing the baseball. Coaches need to emphasize these movements at every practice until the players are establishing the ideal launch position.

To summarize, the preceding pictures demonstrate Chris getting into good fielding position and then developing the ideal launch position using good, quick feet. It's important to understand that these movements are not typical for most position players.

Instead of the jab step (in front) that forces the body to be in line with the target, the typical infielder's move to start the throwing action (even if a good fielding position is achieved) is a swing of the back foot <u>behind</u> the player. When a reverse turning action of the lower body is used in this manner after fielding the ball, it is difficult to achieve consistent alignment of the upper and lower body to the target.

Taking a jab step forward (in front of the player) with the back foot followed by taking the heel of the lead foot toward the target, provides a consistently aligned upper and lower body position. These fielding and throwing mechanics better enable the arm swing to be in line with the body to achieve the ideal launch position as we discussed previously. The reverse lower body swing tends to cause the reverse arm swing to go behind the back.

The first of these next three pictures shows Chris behind the plate in the receiving position that would be used by a catcher with a runner on base. From this starting position, the catcher should receive the baseball and make the same basic forward, square jab step that has just been discussed for the infielder. As you review these pictures,

please note how low Chris stays as he prepares to throw the baseball and how similar the lower body actions are for an infielder and a catcher. The jab step in front with the back foot and corresponding forward movement with the heel of the lead foot are made with the weight on the balls of the feet and the legs in a very athletic position.

From this athletic position, with a significant portion of his weight on his back leg, Chris is ready to generate a maximum amount of rotational energy.

When an outfielder picks up a ground ball or catches a fly ball, the first lower body action is to execute a crow hop, instead of the jab step, to get the back leg into position to throw the baseball. A crow hop for the outfielder consists of a strong leap upward and forward by the lead leg. The outfielder's weight should move in line with the target and the pivot foot should again move in front of the outfielder and land in a square position to the target. This landing position is very similar to the jab step position shown in the pictures above for the infielder and the catcher. After the pivot foot lands square to the target, the heel of the lead leg should go toward the target as we have discussed throughout the book. When the lead foot hits the ground, the elbow should be above the shoulder.

Effectively, what we have just described is the exact same resulting position of the lower body and upper body in the launch position independent of whether the player is a pitcher, catcher, infielder or outfielder. The techniques applied to get into the ideal position may be different, but the launch position that results is the same.

The next picture shows Paul approaching launch with a closed upper and lower body. As we've discussed, this closed position, just before launch, is more difficult to achieve for a position player than for a pitcher because the position player's feet do not always start from a nice square position to the ultimate target. The point of emphasis in this picture of Paul is that the back leg is bent in a very square, athletic position. The knee has not turned toward the target at all.

One significant problem that occurs from a non-square pivot foot is a breakdown or forward turn of the back leg prior to attempting to execute a powerful rotation. This breakdown is evidenced by excessive forward bend in the knee and a non-athletic position for executing a hard, level turn of the hips. I've had several position players exhibit this fault over the years and it tends to be a difficult problem to get the player to correct. It is a very significant fault, though, and should be eliminated in order to create a more powerful throwing action.

The following four pictures of Matt and Chris attempt to demonstrate the breakdown in the back leg that will significantly reduce the player's ability to generate good arm speed. Please contrast the positions of Matt and Chris's back leg with the above picture of Paul just before launch.

These pictures demonstrate the weight drift problem that has been mentioned several times before. In the second picture of Matt, you can see almost all of his weight is on his lead leg and he hasn't started the throwing action yet. The result will be a hard effort with his arm rather than with his legs and trunk.

We can continue to focus on the optimal lower body actions by looking again at the earlier picture of Paul in between the start and the launch positions. The camera angle is in front of Paul to show the position of the lead leg and lead shoulder as we progress toward launch. The emphasis here is to insure the lower body and upper body are slightly closed to the target. The term "closed" means that Paul's back and rear end have a tendency to point to the target rather than his chest and thighs pointing to the target.

One of the best teaching techniques to establish a "closed" upper and lower half is to emphasize taking the heel of the lead foot to the target. Taking the heel, not the toe, to the target prevents the front hip from opening early. The following pictures of Matt and Chris demonstrate two different views of this common fault of having the lead shoulder and hip open early.

Just as it isn't natural for a young player to instinctively have a loose reverse arm swing to "launch," it isn't natural for the player to be closed to the target leading up to "launch."

However, the closed position forces a coil spring action of the upper and lower body that is "wound" at the launch position. If the player starts slightly closed and maintains the closed position to launch, he should be ready to "throw the ball with his legs." This is again a point for coaches to overemphasize or exaggerate, because the natural tendency for most young players is to have the front side very open when the front foot lands. By overemphasizing the front side being closed, the hope is that the player will result in a slightly closed action up until the foot just touches.

ABSOLUTE #7

The lead shoulder and lead leg need to be closed slightly as you approach "launch"...

In summary, then, the most common early lower body action begins with the lead shoulder opening and the toe of the lead foot pointing to the target as shown in the preceding four pictures of Matt and Chris. From this incorrect early position, a large portion of the available rotational energy of the legs has been eliminated and the player is forced to throw the ball almost exclusively with his arm. This throwing technique can place undue stress on the shoulder and elbow and won't achieve optimal velocity.

In listing the most common throwing problems for young players, the three at the top of the list are

1. not getting the elbow above the shoulder,
2. swinging the arm behind the back and
3. opening the front hip and shoulder early.

These three faults are actually tied together because a behind the back, improper arm swing creates a weak position at launch that many times forces the player to open his lead hip and lead shoulder early. The next pair of pictures will attempt to demonstrate this point.

Both of these pictures show the throwing arm in a less than optimal position as Matt and Chris approach 'launch." The palm of the hand is under the ball, possibly the result of an arm swing that went behind the back, as we discussed earlier.

The hand and arm action from this starting point will be unnatural if the lower body is closed to the target as described earlier. If the player starts a hard turn from this less than optimal arm position, the only athletic maneuver that will be comfortable will be to open the lead shoulder and lead hip very early. This characteristic throwing motion is typical of the majority of players that come to me for individual instruction.

So, if the hand is in the palm up or palm forward position at launch, a player's natural tendency is to open the hips and front side early. In order to maximize velocity from this starting position, the good athlete will tend to use his back and chest to snap the upper body forward. This action can create some whip in the arm, but it tends to be less than optimal and it tends to be a more complicated maneuver and more difficult to keep consistent. A fast bending motion of the upper body tends to put stress on the back and causes the throwing athlete to exert an unnatural motion as compared to rotation around the spine. In the following two pictures, Matt and Chris attempt to demonstrate this poor technique of throwing that is characterized by snapping the upper body forward.

CHAPTER 7

THROW THE SAME WAY YOU HIT

One teaching concept for establishing proper lower body throwing technique is to try to get a player to use his legs, hips and back much like he does when he executes good hitting technique (this makes the assumption that he has good hitting technique.) Young players love to go to the field and take their swings and normally players spend a lot of time in the cage hitting. The player needs to be convinced that the same type lower body mechanics are needed to initiate the throwing action and the hitting action. (Most players also need help to understand the value in balancing the amount of time spent working on throwing as well as hitting.)

Both the throwing motion and hitting motion should have the following similar lower body checkpoints.

- a closed launch position with more weight on the back side than on the front side
- the player's weight should be on the balls of the feet throughout the action
- when the stride foot touches the ground, the bat (ball) should be in the "launch" position
- launch begins with a hard turn of the lower body and trunk, not with bat (ball) movement

The first point stresses having the majority of the player's weight on the back leg at launch. This simply continues the concept of an athletic position that enables a hard rotation. If a forward stride is accomplished that takes any substantial portion of the weight to the front leg before the throwing action begins; it will be very difficult to generate a hard lower body rotation (even if the front hip is closed.) The only rotation available will be of the upper body. As was discussed earlier, some whip is achievable with this action, but it will not be the maximum. Nearly all hitting instructors concentrate on

55

minimizing the amount of forward weight transfer prior to initiating the swing.

The second check point listed for the lower body in hitting (and in throwing) is that the player must have his weight on the balls of the feet. A maximum hard turning action cannot be generated with any significant weight on the heels. I generally begin a teaching discussion on this subject by asking a player if he knows why there are two holes that get dug on the mound and in the batter's box during a game. The answer is that skilled pitchers and hitters rotate their hips to throw (or to hit) and as a result they spin on the balls of their feet. Generally, hard rotation is a concept universally taught to hitters, but not really emphasized to throwing athletes. The following pictures of Matt and Chris show the players hitting with these two starting fundamentals implemented very well.

ABSOLUTE # 8

Your weight needs to be on the balls of your feet in order to make a strong hip and trunk rotation…

The third check point for hitters (and throwers) is that the stride foot and the bat (ball) position are timed such that the bat (ball) is ready when the foot touches the ground. For the throwing athlete this means the ball is in the "launch" position before the stride foot touches. Again, this isn't something that is implemented easily. A lot of repetitions are required to achieve the proper timing. It is important for the throwing athlete to know that there is nothing wrong with getting to the proper launch position early.

The next picture shows Paul slightly after the launch position. At this point his legs and hips have begun a hard turn. The important thing to note is that the action begins with the lower body, not with any intentional movement of the throwing hand. In the picture, Paul's throwing hand is still almost in the launch position after the turn has started, even though there is some external rotation in the shoulder that has begun. Careful attention to the picture will note that the left elbow is starting to pull to the rear to aid the upper body in working with the lower body in the turning action. The other point to emphasize is that there is no tilt of the upper body as the turn is begun.

This picture also shows that the weight shift from back side to front side occurs as a result of the hard turn, not due to a shift prior to turning. This is an extremely important point and one that is difficult to get players to achieve.

A common problem young players exhibit is turning the ball early, even after achieving a good launch position. The result of an early turn of the hand is less than optimal acceleration of the arm because the player simply tries to start to throw the ball only with his arm. The concept of starting the action with the lower body is something that takes time for the athlete to master. It isn't the natural action for a player that normally throws the ball exclusively with his arm. The concept of starting the swinging action with the lower body rather than with the hands is one of the more difficult things to get hitters to implement.

Another common problem that throwers exhibit is a tendency to pull the hand in toward the head as the lower body rotation begins. This shortening, or lack of extension, can reduce hand speed. Using the whip analogy, it would be as though you removed some of the length of the whip and the shortened whip will result in reduced tip speed. The push away drill in the back of the book is intended to help correct the tendency to shorten the throwing arm.

Check point four for hitters and throwers, defines the development of a maximum hip turn. The result of the maximum energy legs, hip and trunk rotation for the thrower is a force that causes maximum external rotation of the throwing arm in the shoulder socket. For the hitter, the hard rotation should pull the hands toward the ball, ready for release of the barrel of the bat to the hitting position. The following pictures of Matt and Chris show the power sequence for hitters with the hands pulled forward with the turn and then exploded to the ball with the wrists.

ABSOLUTE # 9

The hand is "whipped" toward the target by a maximal effort, level rotation of the legs, hips and lower back...

After the player has trusted his lower body and trunk to execute a hard turn, he can begin to assist the acceleration of his arm. One of the most difficult aspects of throwing hard is achieving the optimal time to begin working the arm to help the lower body. If the player starts too early, the whip won't be effective and if he starts too late the arm will "drag" and again, not achieve maximum velocity. Because the tendency for all players is to start early with the arm, the focus of training and teaching needs to concentrate on starting the legs and torso first. Again, this is a point of exaggeration in my teaching techniques.

After the examination of the full flex picture of Paul from before, it should be evident that extreme shoulder flexibility is a characteristic of hard throwers and restriction in this joint should be reduced as much as possible. Actually, the player wants a combination of great flexibility in the shoulder and sufficient strength around the shoulder socket. There are many good books that include descriptions of the rotator cuff and discussions of exercises that are recommended for throwing athletes. I've included a discussion of rotator cuff exercises in the Strength and Conditioning segment later in the book.

It's very important to understand that the proper shoulder strength for the throwing athlete is not achieved with curls, triceps work, rows, bench press, etc. The four tendons and associated muscles of the rotator cuff require a very specific set of exercises that typically utilize light free weights below five pounds (or surgical tubing) that emphasize form over effort. Again, there are texts devoted to detail care of the shoulder and it's recommended you add one to your library if your son is a serious baseball player. Proper care and strengthening of the shoulder requires a dedicated workout schedule of 3 to 4 days a week for position players and 7 days a week for pitchers. It is very important to understand that shoulder work isn't just for pitchers. I've had a lot of position players that have needed to improve their shoulder strength in order to maintain throwing health and I always ask players to improve their shoulder strength before working to throw harder.

At this point it has been emphasized that a maximal turning effort is required to create the maximum velocity a player can achieve. The young player needs to understand that the way he will throw the ball as hard as possible is by rotating as hard as possible. A hard rotation offers the potential to achieve the maximum whip of his hand. The throwing drills in this book take players many repetitions to master. Once a player understands the cause and effect as described in the text, he has a good chance to achieve positive results. There is a spin drill and an explosion drill described in the back of the book that attempt to focus on development of a strong turn. These drills are not easy for players to master and then incorporate into the overall throwing motion.

CHAPTER 8

ARM SLOT

The following picture shows Paul at the release point, finishing off the maximal effort of throwing the ball.

Before continuing, it is helpful to understand the relationship between the release point of the baseball and the position the arm attains at launch. Clearly, the goal is to have the palm directed backward with the elbow above the shoulder, just prior to the turn, but there are a lot of different arm positions that satisfy these two criteria. We haven't yet described the bend in the elbow, the amount the elbow is above the shoulder and the relationship of these two elements to the release point.

The position that the arm achieves at launch determines the "arm slot" that the throwing motion attains after the lower body and trunk have generated a hard turn as described previously. "Arm slot" may not be a familiar term, but basically it describes whether a player releases the ball with a sidearm delivery, an overhand delivery or a three-quarter delivery as shown in the adjoining picture of Paul.

The following four pictures are examples of Matt and Chris that show the arm at nearly full extension with the elbow and hand just slightly above the shoulder prior to the turn. After a hard turn, the arm slot is close to sidearm for both players. A sidearm action is not conducive to accurate, true throws for position players, but can create good ball movement for a pitcher. It's important for the coach to try to eliminate a sidearm slot at as early an age as possible.

The next four pictures show examples of a high arm and a high elbow position at launch and present the left handed and right handed release points that result from this launch position (after the hard leg, hip turn). This arm slot is classified as straight overhand. Again, this arm slot is not optimal for best throwing accuracy or velocity.

The following four pictures show both Matt and Chris with their arms with a slight bend in the elbow and more height above the shoulder than in the sidearm pictures but with less than the overhand pictures. In this example, the arm slot that is generated is classified as "three-quarter" as discussed previously. A three-quarter arm slot is between sidearm and straight overhand and is the most accurate and powerful arm slot that a player can achieve. Generally, sidearm throwers can be classified as having trouble locating right and left with pretty consistent up and down control. Overhand throwers have more difficulty managing up and down location but tend to be able to locate well right and left. A three-quarter position arm slot is the best compromise between sidearm and straight overhand.

The preceding pictures show how the arm slot can be adjusted by varying the arm position at the point where the turn is initiated (launch.) This is a very important concept to get across when trying to instruct young players. I certainly believe that the three-quarter arm slot is optimal for accuracy and velocity, but players are difficult to clone perfectly in this regard. That said, in almost all cases a three quarter arm slot can be achieved with a lot of repetitions of the relaxed, reverse arm swing combined with timing of a maximum effort turn.

CHAPTER 9

THE FINISH

After the arm has been accelerated to maximum velocity by the lower body and upper body (assisted by the arm), the finish of the throwing action (after release) needs to concentrate on reduction of as much stress as possible to the arm and shoulder. In order to accomplish this stress reduction, the player needs to take as long (in time) as possible to reduce the speed of the arm from maximum to zero. The path the arm takes during the deceleration process, therefore, needs to be as long (in distance) as possible as shown by the picture of Paul finishing his delivery.

The following two pictures show Matt and Chris after releasing the ball. The throwing arm moves outside the lead leg as the arm slows down. At this point, there is stress being distributed across the shoulder blade and across the back.

An abrupt finish to a maximum effort throwing motion can cause discomfort related to biceps tendonitis. Biceps tendonitis is characterized by a dull pain at the outside top of the shoulder (the attachment point of the biceps tendon). Sometimes the discomfort is localized in the meat of the muscle of the biceps itself. A lot of sidearm throwers suffer from biceps tendonitis because they finish abruptly coming across their body. Some three quarter and overhand throwers can develop biceps tendonitis if they throw against a front leg that is very stiff at the release point. This stiff front leg causes a shorter deceleration time for the arm. An ideal finish position for the end of the throwing action has the front leg with a slight bend to allow the arm more distance and time to decelerate. The thrower bends at the waist after release of the ball and the back leg comes even with or past the front leg as the motion comes to completion. Both of these actions spread the deceleration force across the back rather than focusing it in the outside of the upper arm.

Again, it is easy to conclude from these discussions that we are only talking about pitchers, but the same issues are important for infielders, outfielders and catchers. All position players are prone to biceps tendonitis when they finish the throwing action abruptly.

ABSOLUTE # 10

The throwing motion should finish as long in time and distance as possible...

CHAPTER 10

SUMMARY

This book has been intentionally kept short in order to reduce the steps in the throwing process and therefore maximize the student's ability to understand what is required. A conscious effort has been made to reduce the number of teaching elements as much as possible without omitting critical information. It's important for coaches to understand that most young players can only absorb and retain about three technical points during a teaching session. This book is based on my teaching experience, and has been written to maximize the benefit associated with each teaching step. A deliberate attempt has been made to reduce the total number of teaching steps.

In this book, the critical throwing elements are limited to a total of 10. These fundamentals are summarized below:

- A proper grip uses light pressure of two fingertips on top of the ball and the edge of the thumb on the bottom.
- The throwing action begins with the thumbs and palms of both hands directed downward (throwing hand on top of the ball.)
- The reverse arm swing should stay even or ahead of the shoulders (not behind the back).
- The throwing elbow should be above the shoulder with the palm pointed backward at launch.
- The throwing arm, hand and wrist should be relaxed if the ball is to be "whipped" by the lower body rotation.
- The pivot foot should be square to the target until launch.
- The lead shoulder and lead hip should be slightly closed as launch is approached.
- The majority of the player's weight should be on the back leg and all weight should be on the balls of the feet in order to make a strong hip and trunk rotation.

- The throwing hand will be whipped toward the target by a maximal effort, level rotation of legs, hips, lower back and upper body.
- The throwing motion should finish as long in time and distance as possible.

A solid understanding of these 10 elements and incorporation of the following teaching drills into daily practice sessions will provide the dedicated player an opportunity to maximize his throwing ability.

In addition to these fundamental elements, there are several statements throughout the book that define the overall instructional intent of the author. These are listed below.

- Good throwing technique is not intuitive for most players. The proper steps must be learned and practiced.
- Performance numbers are not important for young players, **TOOLS** are.
- Size and strength ultimately will not be sufficient for success. Excellent technique is required.
- Young players should concentrate on throwing hard, using proper technique.
- Both girls and boys can be taught to throw with good technique.
- A "no pain, no gain" approach for the throwing athlete makes "no sense."
- If you don't fix the problems at the start of the throwing motion, you won't be able to fix the problems at the finish.
- You can't get your arm up into position too early. You can only get there too late.

These concept statements are the essence of a philosophy of "player development." I define player development as "continued improvement day to day, week to week, month to month and year to year." This process is used to develop the best baseball players at all ages.

CHAPTER 11

DRILLS

The following list of drills is in the sequence that I generally use with young players that come to me for instruction. I try to emphasize to all players that the most important aspect of working on throwing is to get started correctly. With that thought in mind, a first teaching session might focus only on the proper grip and the proper arm swing to achieve the correct launch position of the throwing hand. With this instruction, the player is sent home to practice these simple, but critical aspects of throwing. When the player returns in a week or so, I can tell a lot about his disciplined approach to working and his probability of success if we continue to work together. If the player doesn't have a good work ethic, I am generally not enthusiastic about continuing the teacher-student relationship. As has been mentioned often in this book, several years of throwing incorrectly will ingrain muscle memory that can only be changed with a hard-nosed and disciplined work ethic.

One other aspect of instruction that I try to get across during the first session with the player is that the number of repetitions isn't nearly as important as the percent of repetitions that are done correctly. I think most players have the idea that the more times something is done the more improvement they are going to make. By contrast, what the player needs to understand is that he has already thrown the ball thousands of times incorrectly and his body already knows how to do that. Now, his body needs to get the feeling of how to do the action correctly. Any regression back to bad technique is recognized by the muscle memory and reinforced. So, it's much better to do 10 repetitions perfectly than 50 repetitions that might be 50-75% correct. Generally, all players are in a rush to get better. The truly disciplined ones will recognize that it has taken a while to establish the techniques that are being used now and it will take a while to get them corrected. The quality of the practice routines, not the quantity of practice routines, is the key to improvement.

Grip Drill

This drill is excellent for working on the hand position that the player should use on the baseball. The player should spin the baseball, much like snapping the fingers, and then catch the ball with the throwing hand. As quickly as possible (without looking at the ball), the player should get the ball into the ideal grip with the fingers on top (ball out on the fingertips) and the edge of the thumb on the bottom. This is a drill that can be done by the player at home, so a large number of repetitions should be expected. It takes a large number of repetitions for the desired grip to begin to feel normal.

This grip drill is also extremely good for more accomplished players in order to develop the ability to get the proper grip quickly when taking the ball out of the glove. For a catcher, especially, this type of drill is invaluable to establish the proper grip and a quick release to throw runners out. For all players, you want to emphasize that the four-seam grip should be achieved in each repetition.

Thumbs Down Drill

Stage 1

This drill is intended to insure that the player starts the arm swing properly. The player should stand with his feet separated beyond shoulder width with the hands together at the waist and weight on the balls of the feet. The player should separate his hands, thumbs down, and slowly swing both arms to the ideal launch position that has been established previously. At the launch position both the palm of the throwing hand and the palm of the glove hand should face away from the player. The emphasis point for the drill should be to have both arms relaxed throughout the swing while keeping the arms aligned with the shoulders.

Stage 2

After the player establishes a good feel for the relaxed, reverse arm swing with his feet on the ground, he needs to incorporate movement of his lower body into the action. Proper incorporation of the lower body is accomplished by making sure the weight is again on the balls of the feet. He should start by lifting the lead leg and by taking the heel of the lead foot toward the target. Prior to the lead toe touching the ground, the throwing arm should be in the "launch" position. When this thumbs down drill stops, approximately 75-80% of the player's weight should be on the back leg. To achieve an ideal reverse arm swing, the hands will need to separate early (as the knee begins to lift) to get the elbow above the shoulder before the lead foot lands. This later timing requirement needs to be accomplished while still maintaining a slow smooth reverse arm action.

Coaching this drill for young players requires that you do some "hands on" type instruction. You may need to slightly resist the forward movement of the hips, for example, to keep the player's weight back. Typically, you need to work with players to keep the lower body action slowed down so that the arm can get up before the front foot touches. It seems that most players want to rush the lower body and have difficulty in keeping the arms moving quick enough to achieve the correct elbow position.

Wall Drill

This is the best drill I've found to prevent a player from taking his arm behind him during the reverse swing. The player should stand with his heels, lower back and upper back against a solid wall. The lower back and upper back should be against the wall throughout the reverse arm swing (until the arm has reached the launch position.) The solid wall will give immediate feedback to the player when he takes his arm behind him because his knuckles will hit the wall. Sore knuckles have a tendency to offer negative feedback for poor technique. To best implement this drill, the player should actually throw a ball (or some other object) after reaching and holding the launch position for two seconds. The drill needs to be repeated until the player's normal arm action stays parallel with his shoulders.

The reason to suggest that an object other than a ball could be thrown is to give the player an alternative to work on this drill in his home. If the player uses a rolled up pair of socks or some other soft object in place of the baseball, he can work on this wall drill in the house.

There is another method that a coach can utilize to get the point across to a player who is taking his arm behind his back. The coach should stand to the rear of the player's throwing side, at about a 30 degree angle in front of the player. What I ask him to do is exaggerate the reverse arm swing by taking the ball towards me. In effect, asking the player to swing his arm on a line at an angle in front of his body. I use the example of the player steering a large captain's wheel on a boat. As he allows his throwing arm to follow the rotation around the captain's wheel, the arm goes through the exaggerated reverse path in front of his body. Ultimately, the arm swing needs to be in line with the shoulders, but this forward swing exaggeration is a good technique for correcting a behind-the-back maneuver that feels natural to the player.

Spin Drill

This drill is an exercise to increase strength in the rotating muscles of the body and to build a consistent feel for what it takes to make a hard turning action. Make sure your player is thoroughly warm and stretched out prior to starting this dynamic exercise. I would suggest a couple laps followed by stretching and some interval pickups so that a full sweat has been broken. The intent of this drill is to have the player concentrate on only his legs, hips and trunk in attempting to maximize the rotational energy that he can create.

The player needs to have his back several feet from a fence or other object that is directly behind him. His weight should be on the balls of the feet, his hips should be level and his arms outstretched slightly in front of him. The player should focus on a maximum effort, explosive turn to reach the target that is behind him (wall, etc.), then return to the starting position. Again, making sure that the weight is on the balls of the feet and the hips are level to start, he should repeat the drill. It isn't recommended that you do this drill on turf because you will destroy the area where the players turn with their cleats. An ideal location to do the drill is a gravel area where the foot rotation is easily achieved. The pictures of Matt and Chris show the drill being accomplished in tennis shoes on an Astroturf type mat.

As with most muscle building or strengthening exercises, it is best if the athlete attempts to balance the front/back or right side/left side. In order to accomplish this balance in the spin drill, hard turns should be executed both in the throwing direction and the reverse direction. Three sets of 10-15 rotations in each direction should be a good daily goal for your players. This drill emphasizes maximum exertion and will add strength to the major muscle groups of the trunk.

After the player has become comfortable with this maximum effort drill, he can modify it to where the start position has his arms in the "launch" position. Concentration should still be on a totally relaxed arm and a maximum turn without throwing the ball. The player should be encouraged to feel the arm whip forward with the ball in the hand.

Weighted Ball Drill

[CAUTION: A weighted baseball should not be used for throwing hard or throwing long distances. It is used exclusively for rehab after injury and for training as explained here. Use of a weighted ball should be accompanied with rotator cuff exercises as described later in this book.]

This weighted baseball drill is utilized to get the player to better understand three different aspects of throwing after the player has achieved the ideal launch position.

1. establishing the feel of a relaxed arm, from the shoulder to the fingers
2. establishing the feel of starting the throwing action with the legs instead of the arm
3. establishing the feel of reverse rotation in the shoulder socket

I generally start this drill with a 10-ounce baseball and very quickly move to a 7-ounce ball to limit the stress that is applied to the shoulder. The drill begins with the player in the launch position and does not include throwing the weighted ball. The player is instructed to relax the arm and to concentrate exclusively on the lower part of his body. With the weighted ball held in a totally relaxed hand and arm, the player is instructed to execute a reasonably hard turn and to feel the external rotation in the shoulder.

By starting with the 10-ounce ball in the launch position, there is a significant tendency for the ball to stay static in position while the lower body rotates. When the ball stays still as the lower body turns, the upper arm is forced to reverse rotate in the shoulder socket (there are some elementary physics principles at work here.) The reverse rotation in the shoulder socket is extremely important for the player to understand because it is the critical element that allows the baseball to be whipped. External rotation in the shoulder loads energy into the shoulder in a spring-like fashion and this energy is given back to the upper and lower arm in the form of hand acceleration (whip).

As the book has stated several times, this isn't a normal feel for the average player, because he isn't totally in control of throwing the baseball with his arm and hand. In actual fact, when the player utilizes the techniques in this book properly, he doesn't begin to throw the baseball with his arm until the arm has reverse rotated completely in the shoulder socket.

Explosion Drill

This drill emphasizes the lower body as the driving force of the throwing motion. It logically follows the Thumbs Down Drill, the Spin Drill and the Weighted Ball Drill. The player starts with his feet well outside the shoulders with the weight on the balls of the feet. The throwing hand should be in the optimal three-quarter launch position described in the text and the glove hand should be at extension with the palm pointed away. The player begins with his weight slightly shifted to the back foot. At this point, with the knees flexed, the player starts the turning action.

The action is similar to the Spin Drill, as the upper legs, hips, and lower back execute an explosive, level, turn. The turn loads coil type tension of the arm into the shoulder socket which whips the throwing hand toward the target. In theory, a player should be able to execute this drill and throw very close to as hard as he can.

However, this drill is best implemented by throwing the ball no farther than 20-30 feet. I generally work this drill with a bag of baseballs and have the player throw into a net. In this manner he can get a lot of repetitions in a short amount of time. The points that should be stressed are the starting position (ideal launch), a relaxed arm and shoulder, the explosive turn and then a good finish with the back side coming over to where the two feet are even at the end of the throwing action.

To summarize, then, different players have different aptitudes and awareness of their bodies. Generally, it takes a lot of repetitions before a player establishes a good feel for the explosion and the resultant reverse arm torque. Throughout the repetitions, you need to continually emphasize that the explosive motion is strictly rotation.

There shouldn't be any significant forward movement of the upper body until the hard turn has been executed.

Two Piece Drill

This is essentially a combination of Stage 2 of the Thumbs Down Drill and the Explosion Drill and it is intended to make the player focus on each aspect of proper technique. I generally start by having the player count two seconds pause between the Thumbs Down Drill portion and the Explosion Drill portion. Early on, the player should visually check the critical launch position elements before exerting the hard turning action to throw. Most players want to get started throwing quickly, so you need to keep this in mind to emphasize proper mechanics. As the player gains improvement, the two pieces of the action can be allowed to be closer and closer together until they form one fluid throwing motion. Again, a bucket of balls is useful to be able to execute a significant number of repetitions in a short amount of time and the throwing distance should be limited to 20-30 feet.

Another variation of this two piece drill is to have the player get in the launch position and initiate a hard turn without throwing the ball. He should work on establishing the feel of the reverse load in the shoulder socket, then just finish the throwing action with the arm. Essentially, then, the throwing action is being broken into three sections: launch, rotation and release. The release should be emphasized to be three-quarter.

Push Away Drill

This training maneuver is really an extension of the Explosion Drill for a player that is having trouble achieving and maintaining good arm extension. As was mentioned earlier in the book, the palm should continue to face to the rear as the explosion begins and the arm should not be pulled in toward the head.

To begin this drill, the player should get into the launch position with the elbow above the shoulder, palm pointed away and elbow at about a right angle (slightly more to the overhand launch position.) The player wants to concentrate on pushing the palm of his throwing hand away from his head as he begins to rotate with his lower body.

At first, the player can execute the move slowly to make sure the arm is relaxed and moving backward as the rotation begins. As he develops the slow motion feel for the drill, the pace can be quickened.

One test for maintaining good extension is for the coach to stand behind the player and insert his hand between the player's hand and head. If the player is pulling his hand in, he will contact the coach's hand. If the drill is executed with good arm extension, the coach's hand will not be touched when a maximum effort turn is executed. The following pictures shows Matt and Chris demonstrating the position of the player and coach during improper and proper arm action.

Focus Drill (Game of 21)

Although this book is exclusively directed at teaching the mechanics of a powerful throwing technique, I feel there is a need to add some discussion of mental focus associated with throwing accuracy. Generally, for pitchers, coaches always talk about keeping "your eyes on the target." However, when it comes to position players, the concept of target is not normally emphasized.

If I'm working with a group of infielders, I'll ask them where they are looking when they are throwing the ball to the first baseman. Almost invariably, the player will answer "the first baseman." Looking at the first baseman provides the player a target that is approximately 6 feet high and 2 feet wide—not exactly a sharp focal point. Instead, the player should be selecting a point on the first baseman's body that is about the level of the sternum. The target should be no bigger than an inch in size and from the time the throwing player has the ball until it is released, he should be focused on that spot. He obviously needs to practice this at every workout session to ingrain it into his throwing technique.

For catchers (and sometimes position players), throws may be required to be made before the baseman is in position to receive the throw. In this case, the throwing player needs to have a target defined on the fence, field or wall, above the base. Throwing to the base is not a good concept even if you are a catcher throwing out a base stealer. You would like to give yourself as much margin as possible for a less than perfect throw. The baseman has a much better chance of receiving a ball waist high and dropping the tag than trying to pick up an in between hop when he is on the move.

One of the best techniques I've found to improve concentration and accuracy is by playing "21." To play this game, partners face each other about 50-60 feet apart. Two points are scored if a player throws a ball that would hit the partner in the head (if he didn't catch it). One point is scored if a player throws a ball that would hit the partner above the belt and within the outline of the chest. The receiving player awards points and the game ends when one person in the squad gets to 21. Paul and I play this game when we throw outside during the off season and Paul plays it with other pitchers during the season. In order to prevent the dart throwing technique that was described earlier, at least 75% velocity should be required during this accuracy drill.

CHAPTER 12

CONDITIONING AND STRENGTHENING

When Paul was about 15 years old, he and I went to Elon College and spent several hours with Rick Jones, Elon College's head baseball coach at that time (now Coach Jones is the head coach at Tulane University.) Coach Jones is a tremendously nice individual and took the time to explain his approach to pitching mechanics and off-season conditioning. I was able to take a lot of basic ideas from that meeting and over the years I have continued to refine and expand those concepts for application to the players that come to me for instruction.

Off Season Throwing Program

Getting Ready for the Season

Getting a player's arm and shoulder ready for the spring season (for players in cold weather states) is really a pretty simple process, but does require a regimented sequence of controlled throwing, best supervised by an adult. The conditioning process should start in mid-December, aimed at being ready for February high school tryouts or league tryouts (Paul has always started around Christmas day with his throwing program). An early season throwing program takes about 5 weeks to really implement properly, but doesn't take a lot of time each day. The throwing should be accomplished even if the weather is cold. Simply make sure the player has a few layers of light clothing with a nylon outer layer and the temperature should not be a problem.

Starting the first day, the player should throw about 50-60 throws at half speed (throwing nice and easy) at a distance of 50-60 feet (this distance would be typical of players 13 and older.) Keep the throwing distance shorter for younger players, insuring that the level of effort is down around 50%. If you are a mother or father supervising this activity, it should only last about 7-10 minutes, but that time should consist of steady throwing. The pre-season throwing should be performed three days in a row, followed by a day with no throwing. This four-day sequence should be repeated before any changes are made to the distance or time.

The second week of the off season schedule follows the above pattern very closely with three days throwing and one day off, but the time spent throwing should increase to about 12-15 minutes or 75-100 throws total. The distance should be kept around 60-75 feet and the player should still throw in the range of half speed or a little more.

During the third week, the throwing time should stay around 12-15 minutes, but the pace and distance can increase somewhat. Players should not be at maximum effort during this third week of throwing, even though they will probably feel very strong. It is important to continue to take one day off out of every four. During the third week pitchers should begin to lightly spin the baseball every day to condition the associated muscles and tendons.

The fourth and fifth weeks of throwing should expand the time to approximately 20 minutes and the distance to a maximum of 150 feet. (Again, the distance will vary with the age and strength of the player.) The important thing to emphasize is that the majority of the throwing time should be around 75% effort. Again, the player should take one day off out of every four.

With this type of pre-season program, a player's arm should be ready for the spring season after about five weeks of preparation. For Paul, after five weeks he is ready to go on the mound and finish tuning up for the mid-February start of spring training.

Long Toss

After the player has been throwing in the pre-season program for at least two weeks, a long toss segment can be added to the workout program. This long toss day should replace one of the three normal throwing days and should be accomplished at a football or soccer field that is marked off for distance.

The long toss throwing needs to begin with a short running program that is aimed at getting the player loose and to the point that he has broken a sweat. I would recommend a half mile to 1 mile of distance (again, adjusted for the age and condition of the player) followed by 4-5 sprints in the 200 to 400 yard range.

When the player is good and warm, he should begin to throw to further loosen up the arm and shoulder. After a few minutes of close distance throwing, you should throw as you move apart farther and farther. A good estimate is about five throws at each 5-10 yard spacing (depending on the player's age) that is achieved. The total throwing time should only be about 15 minutes and the distance should be increased the whole time. When the player is close to his maximum distance he should only be allowed to throw about five times. The player should cool down by throwing and continually shortening the throwing distance.

All long toss throwing should be executed on level ground and every throw should be made at about 30-40 degrees elevation. In other words, the player should ***not*** be throwing the ball on a line, but rather should be throwing with a significant arc on the flight of the ball. The increased elevation angle helps the player to stretch the shoulder, back and arm muscles and helps to guarantee that the finish of the throwing action is long and pronounced.

This type of long toss program can be included as a workout during the season, but care must be taken to make sure the player's arm isn't tired from strenuous game or practice effort the previous day. In general, today's players do not throw enough to keep their arms healthy and ready for game stress, but it is hard to categorize all players in this manner.

Care of the Shoulder

My younger son Matt was about 16 years old when he was diagnosed as having suffered a subluxation in his throwing shoulder. The injury was caused when a dive was made back into a first base bag with his throwing arm extended. Later, it was determined that the impact with the bag caused the arm to move excessively in the shoulder joint (not technically a dislocation), damaging a portion of the socket surface and creating a tear in the labrum (the cartilage type material that surrounds the joint).

A long period of time was spent trying to rehab and strengthen the shoulder using free weights and the rotator cuff exercises that Matt demonstrates below. When the rotator cuff program was not successful, a more aggressive rehab program was undertaken using a Cybex machine located at UNC Sports Medicine. The Cybex machine added dynamic strengthening exercises to the rehab program and also allowed Matt's shoulder strength to be measured throughout the exercises. None of these rehab efforts proved successful and surgery was finally recommended as the only alternative.

93

Matt's major symptom after the injury was the ability to throw at maximum velocity one day and then need three days as a recovery period before he could throw hard again. During the days after maximum effort, his shoulder and arm felt "dead." The UNC doctors explained that excessive movement in the shoulder joint was causing trauma to the muscles and tendons around the joint and the "dead" time was time the shoulder needed to recover from the trauma of throwing. Due to the labrum tear, Matt was never able to develop sufficient shoulder strength to limit the internal movement.

Needless to say, during this diagnosis, rehab, surgery and additional rehab process, Matt (and I) became all too familiar with the rotator cuff exercises that he demonstrates below.

Rotator Cuff Exercises

In the following strengthening program, the rotator exercises begin with 1 set of 10 repetitions with a 1 pound weight. The exercises increase to 5 sets of 10 repetitions as the player increases strength. After the player is comfortable with 5 sets at the 1 pound weight, the weight can be increased a pound. The 5 sets of exercises are continued with the added weight until the player again is comfortable.

The weight can be increased in increments until 5 pounds of weight is reached. No further increases in the weight should be allowed. I would recommend parents speak with a sports medicine specialist to determine the earliest age for young players to begin these exercises and to determine the optimal weight for players under the age of 15.

Generally, pitchers are instructed to perform rotator exercises every day and it is recommended that position players perform the exercises 4 days per week.

[Note: Perfect form is required to get the most benefit from the following strengthening exercises.]

Shoulder Flexion: Stand erect with the arm and elbow straight down and the back of the hand facing to the front. Raise the straight arm out in front and take it as high as possible. Hold at this level for 1-2 seconds and return the arm to the side. (Repeat)

Shoulder Abduction: Stand erect with the elbow and arm straight with the hand turned palm forward and rotated as far as possible. Raise the arm to the side, keeping the arm straight and the thumb pointed upward, as high as possible. Hold for 1-2 seconds and return the arm to the side. (Repeat)

Supraspinatus: Stand erect with the elbow and arm straight and the hand rotated inward (palm back) as far as possible. Keeping the arm straight and thumb pointing down, lift the arm at a 30 degree angle between the front and side of the body. Raise the hand to eye level and hold for 1-2 seconds. Return the arm to the side. (Repeat)

Horizontal Abduction: Lie on a table on the stomach with the arm hanging straight to the floor with the hand rotated palm forward as much as possible. Raise the arm straight out to the side keeping the thumb pointed upward. Hold the arm at the maximum height for 1-2 seconds and return the arm to the starting position. (Repeat)

 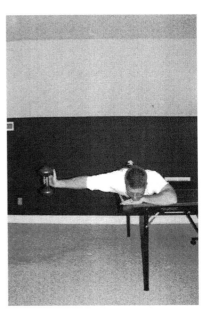

Shoulder Extension: Lie on a table on the stomach with the arm hanging straight down. Rotate the arm palm out with the thumb to the rear. Keep the arm straight and raise the arm backward so the hand is next to your leg or higher (thumb pointed upward). Hold this position for 1-2 seconds and return the arm to the starting position. (Repeat)

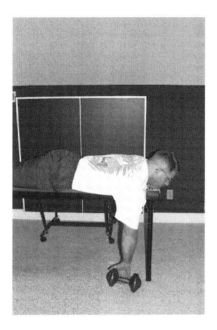 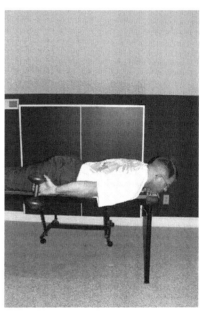

External Rotation: Lie on a table on the stomach with the upper arm held parallel to the table. The hand and forearm should be hanging down with the palm to the rear. Keeping the shoulder and upper arm in place, rotate the hand and forearm even with the table surface or higher (this is the direction of the reverse shoulder rotation that is described in the book). Hold the rotated position for 1-2 seconds and return to the starting position. (Repeat)

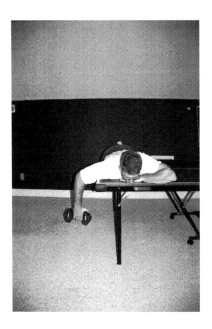 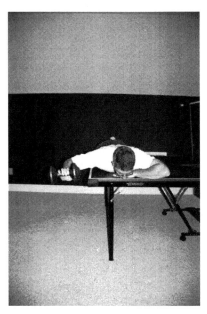

Side External Rotation: Lie on the non-throwing side with the upper portion of the exercising arm held against the side. The elbow should be bent so the palm of the hand is against the stomach. Keep the shoulder and upper arm fixed in place and rotate the hand upward as far as possible. Hold for 1-2 seconds and return to the starting point. (Repeat)

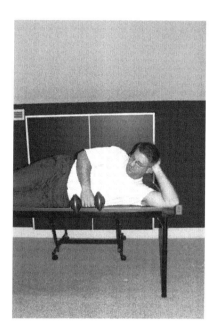 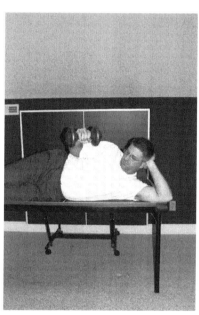

Conditioning

Distance Training

In addition to the rotator cuff strengthening exercises that are included in this section, a discussion of the benefits of distance running to the shoulder (and the rest of the body) needs to be presented. I've been a serious distance runner (average 50 miles per week) for more than thirty years. Over this period of time, I have increased my ability to throw batting practice by a tremendous amount. Now, it isn't uncommon for me to throw batting practice to all the players that try out in the fall of the year. A given tryout day might require 600-800 throws to complete all the 13 through 18 year old players.

I attribute a nearly unlimited ability to throw batting practice (and recover quickly) to a combination of good throwing technique coupled with all the distance running. The repeated swinging action of the arms in the shoulder socket generates a high level of blood flow and creates constant, day after day shoulder exercise. Anyone who is not accustomed to regular distance running knows how tired the arms become if you try to run significantly farther than you are accustomed. This just confirms the effort level associated with the distance work.

This segment is not intended to suggest that young players become distance runners, but it does suggest that there are significant benefits to players who implement a regular running program. The recovery after heavy throwing workouts is just one of the clear benefits of a running program. There are also obvious conditioning benefits to the legs and these benefits show in a player's ability to practice longer and harder.

I've told many of my students and players that baseball isn't a game that requires great conditioning to play (especially position players). However, baseball requires a tremendous number of repetitions to achieve performance improvement. An athlete needs to be in exceptional condition to accomplish high numbers of *quality* repetitions. This is true for throwing, fielding and hitting drills.

Sprint Training

This section is offered in addition to the spin drill in the book to enhance explosive leg action. The importance of sprint drills to build explosive strength in the legs complements the distance training and the work done to increase rotational quickness.

The best technique that I've found for explosive conditioning combines sprints and walking for recovery. To best implement these speed drills, players should be instructed to walk about 10 yards and then sprint 20 yards. At the end of the 20-yard sprint, the player should come to a comfortable stop, turn and walk back to the finish line to again sprint 20 yards. Using this technique the player is effectively walking 20 yards and is sprinting 20 yards. This sequence is repeated 10 times before the sprint distance is increased to 40 yards.

With the sprint distance increased to 40 yards, players should walk about 20 yards before sprinting the 40-yard distance. At the end of the sprint, there should be about 20 yards of deceleration before turning and walking to the finish line to sprint 40 yards again. After 10 repetitions at 40 yards, the player should repeat the 10-yard walk, 20-yard sprint sequence again.

If this sequence of 30 sprint-walk exercises is executed at full out effort, three times a week, a player's leg strength and overall conditioning will significantly increase. A player's corresponding rotational speed in the spin drill will increase. The combination of distance work and explosive sprint work will dramatically improve a player's overall conditioning and therefore, his ability to perform better quality throwing drills. The result will be an ability to throw harder.

William's Flexion Exercises (Care of the Back)

This book emphasizes the need for the player to execute hard rotational turns in order to throw harder. Even though a level rotation should be a safe maneuver for a player, there still is a need to condition and strengthen the back to be able to handle the large number of rotations needed to improve arm speed.

The back exercises that a player should implement are known as William's Flexion exercises. I've personally been doing these exercises daily for the last 20 years. I started doing these after a bout with back problems that were diagnosed as resulting from an imbalance in the strength and flexibility of the hamstrings and quadriceps. This imbalance was coupled with a weakness of the stomach muscles, probably caused by all the distance running.

The solution for the imbalance and weakness was to execute a set of stretches that, over time, would bring the muscles into equilibrium. As a result of the muscles regaining balance, the forces on the back would not be pulling either forward or backward. With good muscle balance and flexibility in the legs, the back should be able to remain in solid alignment. I've found these exercises to be of tremendous benefit over the years.

These William's Flexion exercises do not bring an overnight result, but a consistent, disciplined approach will bring dividends over time.

Pelvic Tilt: This is the first of the concepts to implement and it is performed with the player on his back with the knees bent and the feet on the ground. Starting in this position, the stretch is executed by pressing the small of the back to the floor (stomach tightens and pelvis reverse rotates.) The stretch should be held for 15-20 seconds. As the player becomes more familiar with this stretch, he should attempt to execute it with the legs extended so the back of the knees are touching the floor. Repeat this stretch 5 times.

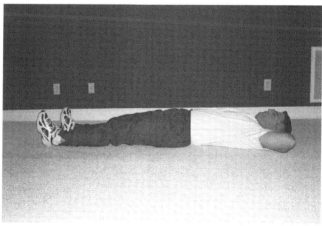

Knees to the Chest: This stretch is an extension of the pelvic tilt just described. With the legs extended and the lower back pressed to the floor, bring one leg up to where the quadriceps is touching the chest with the knee bent. Hold this position for 15-20 seconds. Return the leg to full extension and bring the other leg to where the quad touches the chest (again, the knee is bent). Hold for 15-20 seconds and then bring both legs up to the chest. Hold again for 15-20 seconds. For all three of these stretches the lower back should stay on the floor. As you gain more flexibility in the hamstrings you will be able to get the quads closer to the chest. Repeat this stretch 5 times.

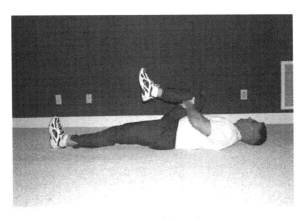

Knees to the Floor: This is a rotational stretch that starts with the player on his back with his hands behind his neck and elbows touching the floor. The player's knees are bent and his feet are on the ground. The right leg is lifted so the outside of the right knee can cross to the outside of the left knee and pull the left knee to the floor. During this stretch the elbows should stay on the floor so the spine will be in torsion. Hold the stretch for 15-20 seconds before switching to pull the right knee with the left knee. Again, hold the stretch for 15-20 seconds with the elbows maintained on the floor. Repeat this stretch 5 times.

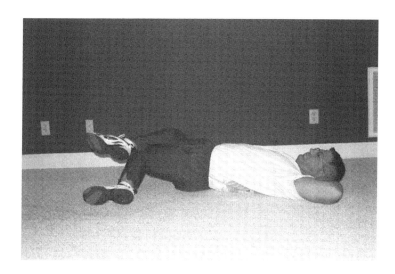

Figure Four: This stretch is executed in the seated position with the left leg extended and the sole of the right foot against the inside of the left knee (right knee bent). Keeping the small of the back as straight as possible, the stretch is executed by taking both hands to the toes on the left foot.   Hold the stretch position for 15-20 seconds. Continue the Figure Four stretch by switching to where the right leg is straight and the left leg is bent with the sole of the foot to the inside of the right knee. Again, keep the back straight and take both hands to the toes on the right foot. Hold this position for 15-20 seconds. Repeat this stretch 5 times.

Groin Stretch: While still in the seated position, bend the knees so the soles of the feet touch together. Pull the feet along the floor toward you. In this position, keep the small of the back straight and reach with both arms straight out in front of you as far as possible. Hold this position for 15-20 seconds and return to the starting point. Repeat this stretch 5 times.

Cat Stretch: For this stretch, the player gets on his hands and knees and arches his back upward as far as possible while he tucks his chin in toward his chest. The stretch is held 15-20 seconds and then the back is arched in the opposite direction with the stomach forced to the floor and the head tilted back as far as possible. Hold this position 15-20 seconds. Repeat each of the stretches 5 times.

Body Rotation: This is the last of the back stretches and begins with the player laying flat on his stomach on the floor with arms and legs extended fully. The stretch begins by raising the left leg and right arm simultaneously. The leg and arm should be straight and both should be lifted as high as possible. Hold the position for 15-20 seconds and return to the starting position. Switch to lift the right leg and left arm simultaneously as far as possible and hold the position for 15-20 seconds. Return to the starting position. Repeat each of these exercises 5 times.

Weight Lifting

One of the major concerns I have with players in the 14-18 year old age range is their tendency to fall in love with weight lifting. There are still a lot of strength coaches that expect baseball players to train exactly the same as the football players; that is, the more weight the better in all lifts. It is my opinion that throwing athletes need to be very careful about the lifting that they do relative to the shoulder joint. I do not like to see players maximizing their effort on the bench press, the military press, overhead pull downs or upright rows. These exercises, if they are going to be done at all, should be performed with relatively light weight. The goal should only be to achieve a level of toning, rather than significantly increasing strength.

The problem with heavy weights and these exercises is that the shoulder joint is being stressed to the extreme. The bench and military press put forces to push the shoulder down and back out of the socket while the pull downs and rows attempt to pull the shoulder out of the socket to the top and front. Any of these exercises can cause impingement or other injury to the throwing athlete if done with very heavy weight.

If injury does not occur, the large muscles in the chest and back will gain mass and shoulder flexibility will be reduced as a result. For throwing athletes, weight training should focus on lower body and trunk strength and quickness.

Weight training can be implemented to strengthen the biceps, triceps, forearms and wrists, but even these exercises should concentrate more on toning than maximum mass building. As the book states several times, velocity in throwing the baseball is achieved with relaxed, flexible muscles that can be whipped by a strong and quick lower body and trunk.

APPENDIX

The following pages show sequences of photographs of Paul's pitching mechanics from three different angles. The photos are from spring training games and were taken by Mr. Kenneth Carr of Cleveland, Ohio.

The first sequence is viewed from a location behind first base and this angle allows a clear view of Paul's back. From this view, most of the elements of the long, loose arm swing are very clear. This view also provides the best angle to see how Paul's weight is controlled. Using this viewing angle, a coach can recognize the player that is getting his weight to the front side too early and consequently isn't achieving a strong launch position.

The second sequence is viewed from a location behind third base and this angle shows a clear view of Paul's chest. From this view, the hands are in view and the start of the action is very clear. In addition to the hand break and early arm action, the player's eyes can be seen to determine if he is consistently looking at the target throughout the throwing motion. This view is also very useful in determining whether the player is lifting or swinging his lead leg to start the throwing motion. The 3rd base view is important to determine how softly the player is landing on his front leg.

The third sequence of pictures is viewed from the front and slightly to the 3rd base side of home plate. This view provides the best opportunity to determine the arm slot that is being used to throw the baseball and allows the spin of the ball and movement on the throws to be seen the best. In addition, this home plate viewing angle allows the closed or open condition of the upper and lower body to be determined. The upper body tilt away from vertical is best seen from this angle and the energy developed from rotation is best determined by viewing the player from the front. The last item that can be best evaluated from the front view is the length of the finish of the arm swing.

Earlier in the book the concept of teaching yourself to see discussed being able to stop the player's movements in frames using your mind. These photo sequences show the critical views and points in time that you need to work on to determine your player's throwing technique. Many of these stop action shots are stopping a very fast moving action that is difficult for your mind to capture. It takes a lot of practice to become proficient at making yourself simulate a 35-mm camera.

View From First Base

A BALANCED START IS DEMONSTRATED WITH GOOD FLEX IN THE BACK LEG, LIFT IN THE LEAD LEG AND EYES ON THE TARGET.

THE HANDS SEPARATE EARLY WITH THE THUMBS DOWN AND WITH THE WEIGHT STAYING BACK RATHER THAN DRIVING FORWARD.

THE REVERSE ARM SWING CONTINUES IN A
SMOOTH ARC WITH THE THROWING HAND
ON TOP OF THE BALL. THE BODY STAYS
CLOSED TO THE TARGET AND WEIGHT
STAYS BACK.

THE LAUNCH POSITION HAS THE BODY
SQUARE TO THE TARGET, HIPS LEVEL,
WEIGHT ON THE BALLS OF THE FEET, ELBOW
EVEN OR ABOVE THE SHOULDER AND PALM
POINTED BACK.

AN EXTREMELY HARD TURN CAUSES THE
ARM TO ROTATE IN THE SHOULDER SOCKET,
THE KEY TO WHIPPING THE BALL TOWARD
THE TARGET.

THE ARM WHIP MAXIMIZES THE RELEASE
VELOCITY OF THE BALL AND A BEND IN THE
FRONT LEG HELPS PROVIDE FOR A LONG
FINISH.

A MAXIMAL EFFORT THROWING ACTION REQUIRES A LONG FINISH OF THE THROWING ARM, OUTSIDE THE LEAD LEG, TO HELP REDUCE THE STRESS ON THE ARM AND SHOULDER.

COMPLETION OF THE MAXIMAL EFFORT THROWING ACTION IS SHOWN BY THE CONTINUATION AND FOLLOW THROUGH OF THE HARD ROTATION.

View From Third Base

A BALANCED START TO THE THROWING ACTION SHOWS A CLOSED LOWER AND UPPER BODY AND FLEX IN THE BACK LEG.

THE GLOVE HAND AND THROWING HAND SEPARATE EARLY AND START THUMBS DOWN. THE WEIGHT STAYS BACK.

AS THE RELAXED ARM SWING CONTINUES IN A SMOOTH ARC, THE HEEL OF THE LEAD FOOT IS TAKEN TOWARD HOME PLATE.

THE MAXIMUM EFFORT TURN IS NEARLY COMPLETE AS THE ARM IS BEGINNING TO ROTATE IN THE SHOULDER SOCKET. THE HIPS REMAIN LEVEL.

A COMBINATION OF SHOULDER FLEXIBILITY AND STRENGTH IS REQUIRED TO ALLOW FULL REVERSE ROTATION IN THE SHOULDER SOCKET.

THE MAXIMUM VELOCITY RELEASE IS DEVELOPED FROM A MAXIMAL ROTATION EFFORT BY THE LOWER AND UPPER BODY.

THE THROWING ARM TRAVELS OUTSIDE THE
LEAD LEG AS THE FINISH OF THROWING
ACTION CONTINUES.   THE BACK LEG IS
PULLED FORWARD BY THE HARD ROTATION.

THE ARM FOLLOWS THE LONGEST PATH
POSSIBLE TO REDUCE THE DECELERATION
FORCE ASSOCIATED WITH SLOWING THE
ARM DOWN.

View From Home Plate (3*ᴿᴰ* Base Side)

THE THROWING ACTION BEGINS WITH A CLOSED UPPER AND LOWER BODY.

THE HANDS BREAK EARLY AND START THUMBS DOWN. THE BODY REMAINS CLOSED TO THE TARGET.

THE BODY CONTINUES CLOSED TO THE TARGET AS THE ARM SWING STAYS IN LINE WITH THE BODY.

THE WEIGHT STAYS BACK AND UPPER AND LOWER BODY STAY CLOSED AS THE ACTION CONTINUES.

THE HEEL OF THE LEAD FOOT IS TAKEN TO THE TARGET AND THE REVERSE ARM SWING DOES NOT GO BEHIND THE BACK.

THE LAUNCH POSITION HAS THE WEIGHT ON THE BALLS OF THE FEET (NOTE THAT THE EYES HAVE NEVER LEFT THE TARGET).

THE MAXIMUM EFFORT LOWER BODY AND UPPER BODY ROTATION GENERATES REVERSE ROTATION OF THE ARM IN THE SHOULDER SOCKET.

THE IDEAL ARM SLOT IS THREE-QUARTER FOR THE OPTIMAL COMBINATION OF VELOCITY AND ACCURACY.

Index

ABOUT THE AUTHOR

Ken Shuey has a master's degree in electrical engineering coupled with thirty-three years of practical experience in the design and development of electronic equipment. He holds twenty-nine patents on a variety of subjects related to his work experience with aircraft electrical systems and communications. Ken grew up playing youth baseball in Missouri and played four years of collegiate baseball at the University of Missouri at Rolla, joining the UMR team for the inaugural season that baseball was offered as a varsity sport. He played several years of post-collegiate baseball in the mid-Ohio area. Ken is the president of the North Wake County Baseball Association, a non-profit organization that provides baseball opportunities for players in the Raleigh-Durham-Chapel Hill area of North Carolina. He is the co-founder of the Greater Raleigh Fall Baseball League (GRFBL), recognized as one of the premier competitive fall baseball programs in the country. Ken is the father of Paul Shuey, setup man for the Cleveland Indians and one of the hardest throwers in the major leagues. Paul's fastball has been clocked as high as 100 MPH and his split finger fastball consistently registers 90-94, one of the hardest in the major leagues. Ken has been providing throwing instruction for dedicated NWCBA players for many years. It is the combined experience of working with Paul and with a variety of NWCBA players, coupled with a strong engineering background, that has allowed a refined set of powerful throwing techniques to be developed.

9163823R0

Made in the USA
Lexington, KY
03 April 2011